THE

DATHAVANSA

THE

DATHAVANSA

OR

THE HISTORY OF THE TOOTH - RELIC

OF

GOTAMA BUDDHA

TRANSLATED INTO ENGLISH, WITH NOTES

MUTU COOMARA SWAMY

GYAN

Published by

GYAN

Gyan Publishing House
5, Ansari Road
Daryaganj, New Delhi-110002
Phone: 011-47034999, 9811692060
E-mail: books@gyanbooks.com

Distribution Network
gyanbooks.com
India, USA, Canada, UK, Australia, France

ISBN : 978-81-212-9230-6 (PB)
First Published, 1874

2nd Impression 2023

Printed at: Gyan Press, Delhi.

TTHE DATHAVANSA
Translator: MUTU COOMARA SWAMY

THE DATHÁVANSA.

Works by the same Author.

ARICHANDRA;

OR,

THE MARTYR OF TRUTH: A DRAMA.

Translated from the Tamil, and Dedicated to the Queen.

SMITH, ELDER, & CO.

SUTTA NIPÁTA;

OR,

THE SERMONS AND DISCOURSES OF GOTAMA BUDDHA.

A Translation from the Páli.

TRÜBNER & CO.

[*To be published at once.*

TÁYUMÁNAVAR,

OR,

HINDU PHILOSOPHIC POEMS OF THE *VEDÁNTIC-SIDDHÁNTIC* SCHOOL.

A Translation from the Tamil.

[*In the Press.*

THE DATHÁVANSA;

OR,

THE HISTORY OF THE TOOTH-RELIC

OF

GOTAMA BUDDHA.

TRANSLATED INTO ENGLISH, WITH NOTES.

BY

MUTU COOMÁRA SWÁMY,

MUDELIÁR,

BARRISTER-AT-LAW, LINCOLN'S INN;
MEMBER OF THE LEGISLATIVE COUNCIL, CEYLON; FELLOW OF THE
ROYAL ASIATIC SOCIETY, LONDON; AND MEMBER OF THE ASIATIC SOCIETY, PARIS.

LONDON:
TRÜBNER & CO., 57 & 59 LUDGATE HILL.
1874.

TO THE RIGHT HONOURABLE

THE EARL OF CARNARVON,

SECRETARY OF STATE FOR THE COLONIES.

My Lord,

In memory of the late Duke of Newcastle, who once so ably presided over the Government of Her Majesty's Colonies, as also in grateful recognition of the services rendered by you and your zealous coadjutors in the Colonial Office, in the cause of furthering the material and moral improvement of the native inhabitants of one of Great Britain's most important Eastern Colonies, Ceylon, I beg to dedicate this work of Oriental learning to your Lordship.

I am,

Your obedient Servant,

MUTU COOMÁRA SWÁMY.

London, *May* 5, 1874.

INTRODUCTION.*

The importance of the study of the Páli language is now fully recognised by Oriental scholars. Its title to distinction has of late been made to rest on the fact of its being the repository of the teachings of the founder of Buddhism. Its value, however, is much wider. To all interested in antiquarian inquiries, whether these relate to religion, philosophy, history, or sociology, Páli literature offers a wide field for research. And as regards the ancient history of India, it will be useless to attempt to elucidate it fully till the resources of the Páli are thoroughly ransacked. To convey a faithful and interesting picture of the deeds and thoughts of the old Hindus, a study of the Tipitaka and Játakas in this language is quite as necessary as that of the Vedic and Puranic Scriptures in Sanskrit. And if the literature found in the former is not as varied as in that of the latter, yet it is equally, if not more, extensive. Nevertheless, whilst every facility may now be obtained for the prosecution of the study of the Sanskrit, the difficulties in the way of the Páli student are very disheartening. A simple and scientific grammar has yet to be published. That valuable contribution to Oriental learning, Professor Childers' dictionary, remains to be completed. As to the text-books printed, their number is exceedingly limited. The beginner is therefore left to resort to the intricacies of the native grammarian, such as Kachcháyana, or to trust himself to the

* For the use of those who may not care to read the original in the Páli, and yet wish to consult its translation into English, the latter alone is embodied in this copy.

incomplete works of Clough or Mason, for acquiring the first principles of the language. And if he wishes to ascertain the meaning of terms, his chief resource as yet is the native glossary of Abhidhánappadípiká, the arrangement of which prevents its being easily utilised. In addition to this, were he called upon to decipher also the caligraphy of Páli words as they are found inscribed on palm leaves, it would certainly entail upon him an unnecessary waste of time, temper, and labour. The text of Dá*th*ávansa, or the "History of the Tooth-Relic" of Gotama Buddha, is printed now for the first time, with the object of removing, to a small extent at least, some of these difficulties. To make it more widely useful, a close and literal translation is also presented in this volume. The aim has been to render the original almost word for word, and to sacrifice elegance rather than correctness, whenever the one was incompatible with the other, and thus to present, even to the general reader, Eastern ideas only in the quaint forms and expressions of the East. Some of the liberties, however, which it was indispensable to adopt in a translation, are specified below.*

Páli, otherwise called Mágadhí, was once the language of a tract of country to the north of the sacred city of Benares,

* 1. Expletives so frequently repeated, yet very natural in Oriental tongues, have been in some cases omitted in the translation as unnecessary.

2. The too frequent use of the demonstrative pronouns has been avoided by rendering them sometimes into the English definite article, to which in truth they often correspond in Eastern languages.

3. Very long sentences, made to depend on a string of past participles, have in some cases been divided into two, and of the participles many converted into finite verbs.

4. Past participles, which sometimes read badly in a translation, have been changed into present participial forms.

5. Connecting terms, such as "and," "his," "their," &c., have often been inserted, when such were unnecessary in the original.

6. Sometimes a little laxity was also required in the rendering of compound adjectives.

7. *Ádi*, occurring so often, and meaning "and such like," has been rendered in various ways to suit the context, and thereby monotony has been to some extent avoided.—*Vide* Note 19, Chap. I.

now more or less defined by the limits of modern Behar. The country itself in which it was spoken was called Mágadha, the birth-land of Buddhism, and the scene of many a momentous event in ancient times. When the religion of the great Indian Reformer was expelled from Hindustan, Mágadhí itself ceased to flourish there, and found its home in the island of Ceylon, and in the Siamese and Burmese kingdoms in the Malayan peninsula. Whilst in some of the countries to which Buddhism had spread, both its tenets and its language became encrusted with the local peculiarities, in Ceylon, from its insular position, the Páli language still retained much of its purity. But more than this, it was always cultivated there with great assiduity. Even now it has a small array of native scholars, though naturally there is not that encouragement to its study which once existed under the native sovereigns.

As "Dáthávansa" is a book held in great estimation, not only by the Páli literati of the island, but also by the Sinhalese priesthood and laity, from its recounting the history of the founder of their religion, it may claim some attention from the learned. Its value is threefold—literary, religious, and historical. It is perhaps one of the finest specimens of Páli poetry extant. A translation can give but a very faint conception of the stern simplicity and chasteness of its style, much less of the sweet rhythm of its metre. It is not indeed so much the ideas themselves, as the elegance of the diction in which they are clothed, that charms equally the native student and his teacher. There is no attempt at ornate and laboured diction or high-flown metaphor. The Nalopákhyán is its worthy equal in Sanskrit in this respect. It is considered so free from faults as to form the text-book for lectures illustrating the grammatical constructions of the Páli language, whilst the flow of words is so attractive, that the whole, or considerable portions of it, are committed to memory by students.

A history of the tooth-relic of Buddha naturally excites much interest in a country where the relic itself is believed to be at present lodged in a shrine which is periodically exposed to admiring crowds, and commands the worship of masses of Buddhists. In truth, the island of Ceylon, or, as it was called of yore, Lanká, "the resplendent," derives an additional title to the reverence of all Eastern nations from their belief in the tooth-relic being now found in the Máligáwa (temple) at Kandy, the seat of the last native dynasty. Only the other day, the ambassadors from Burmah, returning from Europe, appeared in state before the shrine there, in fulfilment of the special commands of their king, and offered it many tokens of obeisance and devotion. Till within a few years the British governors of the island were its special guardians, and their representatives in Kandy had charge of the keys of the sanctuary in which the relic was deposited. It was the belief of the Buddhists that ascendancy in the island belonged to those who had the possession of it, and for some time it was found necessary to humour them in this belief. Though now, owing to the remonstrances of the Christian societies in England, the connection of the existing Government with the shrine has ceased, yet its worship amongst the people,—to whom, the higher teachings of Buddhism being unknown, this relic of idolatry, so repugnant to the genius of Gotama himself, remains the sole symbol and substance of faith,—is kept up with a considerable degree of state and splendour out of the revenues derived from extensive lands and estates with which the temple had been endowed in olden times by the Sinhalese sovereigns.

This work throws some light on the history of India immediately after the date when Buddha died or attained his *Parinibbána*, the state of extinction, as his votaries term it. This would be about two thousand five hundred years ago. The struggles between Brahmanism and Buddhism for ascendancy in some parts of India, especially in Kalinga in the south and Patna in the north, are here duly chronicled. And according to Turnour, though his rendering has been questioned by other scholars, the inscription on the famous columns at Delhi emanated from the "King of kings," or the emperor of all India, referred to in this work as Pá*nd*u, who held his sway at Pá*t*aliputra (modern Patna), and whose conversion to Buddhism is duly recorded here. To establish his theory, that learned Páli scholar gave in one of the early numbers of the *Bengal Asiatic Society's Journal* a brief analysis of this book, with a translation of some of the verses of the third chapter relating to Pá*nd*u. The inscriptions in question are so interesting as to justify one of them being reproduced in a note below.* The spirit of universal charity and philanthropy which animated this edict is not unworthy of the consideration of the present enlightened rulers of the great Indian Empire.

The important part which a belief in miracles played in the propagation of Buddhism amongst the masses is also seen from this book. To the Hindu mind nothing can be more loathsome than the idea of worshipping a relic. And yet miracles, it is recorded here, overcame both reason and prejudice. Thus as a contribution also to the history of miracles,

* *The inscription pointing west.*—"The Raja Pandu, who was the delight of the Dèwos, has thus said : This inscription on *Dhammo* is recorded by me in the twenty-seventh year of my inauguration. My public functionaries intermingle among many hundred thousands of living creatures, as well as human beings. If any one of them should inflict injuries on the most alien of these beings, what advantage would there be in this my edict? (On the other hand) should these functionaries follow a line of conduct tending to allay alarm, they would confer prosperity and happiness on the people as well as on the country; and by such a benevolent procedure they will acquire a knowledge of the condition both of the prosperous and of the wretched ; and will, at the same time, prove to the people and the country that they have not departed from *Dhammo.* Why should they inflict an injury either on a countryman of their own or an alien? Should my functionaries act tyrannically, my people, loudly lamenting, will be appealing to me ; and will appear also to have become alienated (from the effects of orders enforced) by royal authority. Those ministers of mine who proceed on circuits so far from inflicting oppressions, should cherish the people, as the infant in arms is cherished by the wet-nurse ; and those experienced circuit ministers,

the student may find this book a not uninteresting manual. Ample allusion is here likewise made to Nágas, a species of human beings endowed with the hoods of snakes. Somehow they are made to occupy an important place in all the legends and religions of India. In this book they appear as competitors with some of the inhabitants of India for the possession of the tooth-relic of Buddha. From it also we find how unaltered some of the usages of the Hindus are. Many of the customs, rites, and ceremonies described in this book are prevailing up to this day unchanged. Some information on the ancient geography of India may also be gleaned from it. Special mention is made of the Temple at Dantapura—the "Tooth City"—in Kalinga. It may here be of interest to make some extracts from Mr Fergusson's article in the *Asiatic Society's Journal* (Great Britain and Ireland) for 1867, to show the connection which existed between the places and events described in Dáthávansa and the famous *Amrávati Topes*, which have formed the principal theme of a work by him on Indian art, and the remains of which were exhumed by the exertions of Colonel Mackenzie and Sir Walter Elliot. The beautiful photographs, which form such an attraction in that book, are from fragments now in the possession of the India

moreover, like unto the wet-nurse, should watch over the welfare of my child (the people). By such a procedure, my ministers would ensure perfect happiness to my realm.

"By such a course, these (the people) released from all disquietude, and most fully conscious of their security, would devote themselves to their avocations. By the same procedure, on its being proclaimed that the grievous power of my ministers to inflict tortures is abolished, it would prove a worthy subject of joy, and be the established compact (law of the land). Let the criminal judges or executioners of sentences (in the instances) of persons committed to prison, or who are sentenced to undergo specific punishments, without my special sanction, continue their judicial investigations for three days, till my decision be given. Let them also, as regards the welfare of living creatures, attend to what affects their conservation, as well as their destruction : let them establish offerings : let them set aside animosity.

"Hence those who observe, and who act up to our precepts, would abstain from afflicting another. To the people also many blessings will result by living in *Dhammo.* The merit resulting from the charity would spontaneously manifest itself."—*Turnour on the inscriptions on the columns at Delhi, &c.*

Museum, in London. Mr Fergusson, after referring to the sources of information derived from Chinese and Brahmanic authorities regarding these topes, writes :—

"This account, being derived from Brahmanical sources, would hardly help us much; but, fortunately, we have two Buddhist accounts of the same transaction, which are much more complete and detailed, and which do, I fancy, throw great light on our researches. The first is contained in the Daladâ Wanso, partially translated by the Hon. G. Turnour, and published in the J. A. S. B., vol. vi., p. 856, *et seq.;* the other is abstracted by Colonel Low from the Siamese Phrâ Pat'hom, and published in the same journal, vol. xvii., part ii., p. 82, *et seq.* Unfortunately, neither work has been completely translated, and the extracts having been made with reference to other objects, do not give us all the information we want. The following abridgment of the story will, however, suffice for present purposes :—

"The left canine tooth of Buddha had been preserved in Dantapura, the capital of Kalinga, probably at or near Udayagiri, for 800 years, when Gûhasîwo, the king, early in the fourth century, was converted to Buddhism from the Brahmanical faith, which he had professed up to that time. With the zeal of a convert he dismissed and persecuted the Brahmans, who had hitherto enjoyed his favour. They repaired to Pâtaliputta (Patna) to complain of this to the paramount sovereign, here called Pâṇdu, but who, as it appears from the context, most probably was the Gautama Putra of the Satkarṇi dynasty. He orders Gûhasîwo to repair to his court, bringing the relic with him. It is then subjected to every sort of trial. It is smashed on an anvil, thrown into the gutter, and everything conceivable done to destroy or dishonour it. It comes triumphantly out of all its trials. The king is converted, and finally devotes himself to a religious life.

"While all this is going on, a northern king—it is not quite clear whence he came—named Khîrâdhâro, attacks the capital, in order to possess himself of the wonder-working relic. He was defeated and killed in battle, and Gûhasîwo returned, it is said, with the sacred tooth to his capital. Some time afterwards the nephews of Khîrâdhâro, allying themselves with other kings, march against Gûhasîwo. He, though seeing that resistance is hopeless, prepares for defence; but, before going to the combat, he enjoins on his daughter Hemamâlâ, who was married to a prince of Oujein, called Danta Kumâra, that in the event of his falling they should take the relic, and escaping by sea, convey it to Mahâsena, king of Ceylon, who had been for some time negotiating for its purchase.*

"The prince and princess fly from the city before its fall, bury the relic in the sand, in the same manner as the image of Juggernath is said to have been concealed in the Brahmanical account; and afterwards returning, the princess conceals it in her hair, and escaping to the coast, they take ship apparently at Tamralipi or Tamlook, and sail for Ceylon. Half-way between the place of embarcation and Ceylon they are shipwrecked, at a place called the Diamond Sands.† From the context I do not think there can be much hesitation in fixing this locality on the banks of the Kistnah. First, from its position half-way;‡ next, because here only, so far as I

* Some years ago Dr Bird opened a small tope in front of the Kanheri Caves in Salsette. In it he found a copper plate recording that a canine tooth of Buddha had been deposited there. The plate is dated in the year 245. From the expression "Samvat" being used, Dr Stevenson (J. B. B. R. A. S., vol. v., p. 13) assumes that it must be from the era of Vikramaditya. I believe, however, it is correct to assert that no Buddhist inscription is dated from the era of the hated opponent of their religion. If, on the other hand, we assume the era of Salivahana, it brings the date to almost the exact time—A. D. 324—of these events on the east coast; and though it is not directly stated in the inscription, it seems that the tooth was deposited there by Gotami-putra, the very king who played so important a part in the narrative just recorded; and what is more, it seems extremely probable that the Kanheri tooth was, or was supposed to be, the identical one which performed so many miracles in Pâtaliputta.

This might seem paradoxical had not the same thing happened to the same relic in similar circumstances, more than twelve centuries afterwards. When the Portuguese conquered Ceylon, Constantine de Braganza seized the Daladâ and conveyed it to Goa. The king of Pegu sent an embassy after it, and offered any amount of ransom for it. But the bigotry of the priesthood was proof against any such temptation. The tooth was consumed by fire in presence of the Archbishop and all the notables, and the ashes cast into the sea. The result was peculiar. The Ceylonese pretended that the one so destroyed was a counterfeit. A true one was discovered and sold to the king of Pegu, and as soon as he was gone and had paid for it, another true one was found concealed in Ceylon, and is probably the crocodile's tooth that is now so honoured in that country. To complete the parallelism, both the Burmese and the Concani teeth have disappeared, and only their empty chaityas remain. The Ceylonese tooth still remains, with the oldest pedigree of any such relic that the world possesses.

The particulars of this second great attempt to destroy the Daladâ will be found well stated in Sir E. Tennent's Ceylon, vol. ii., p. 199. Translations of the original authorities are there given also.

† *Dinne* means sandbank in Telugu. This may be the origin of the name Dîpal dinne, which certainly does not mean "Hill of Lights." Can Dîpal, by any synonysm, be assumed to mean diamond?

‡ The Siamese, as Colonel Low points out, wishing to make their own country the scene of these events, have lengthened the periods of the voyage preposter-

know, are those diamond * mines near the coast; but more because it was the residence of the Nâga Râja.

"The Nâga Râja steals the relic from the princess, when she is asleep. He is forced by the power of a Thero, from the Himalaya, to restore it, and the wanderers again embark, and after various adventures, reach Ceylon in the year 312.† Mahâsena had been dead nine years, but the fugitives are received with open arms by Meghavarṇa,‡ the reigning sovereign; a brick and mortar Chaitya is made, and the relic brought by the prince and princess enshrined with great solemnity (Col. Low, p. 86).

"The narrative then proceeds:—'Three years had passed away, when the king of Lankâ perceived from an ancient prophecy that, in seven years from that date, a certain king, Dhammasoka Râja, would erect a temple on the Diamond Sands; and he likewise recollected that there were two Donas of relics of Buddha still concealed in the country of Nâga Râja. He therefore directed a holy person to go and bring these relics.' The Nâga Râja's brother swallows the relics, and flies to Meru, but they are taken from him and brought back. 'Soon after this Nâga Râja arrived, in the form of a handsome youth, and solicited a few relics from his majesty, which were bestowed upon him accordingly.'

"His majesty now ordered a golden ship to be made. It was one cubic long, and one span broad. The relics were put into a golden cup; this was placed in a vase, and the whole put into the golden ship. A wooden ship was next built, having a breadth of beam of seven long cubics.

"Danta Kumâra and Hemamâlâ being desirous of revisiting their country, the king of Lankâ sent with them ambassadors to one of the five § kings who now ruled there, requesting him to show them every attention. The vessel reached the Diamond Sands in

---

ously. They make it three months from Cuttack to the Diamond Sands, and three more from thence to Ceylon.—J. A. S. B., vol. xvii., pp. 86, 87.

* One of the objects of Colonel Mackenzie's surveys was to mark the diamond mines in the locality. He plots the diamond district as extending to about eight miles north of Amravati, but it seems there are no mines elsewhere.

† It does not seem quite clear how far the Ceylonese dates are to be relied upon as quite correct about this time. Avowedly there is an error to the extent of at least sixty years in the date their annals assign to Asoka. This has subsequently been adjusted, to some extent, by Mr Turnour, but not, so far as I can judge, in such a manner as to inspire entire confidence. My impression is that the dates in the fourth century are all from ten to fifteen years too early.

‡ Is not this the Varaja of the Western-Cave Inscrip., J.B.B.R.A.S., vol. v., p. 42?

§ Those who, according to the Daladâwanso, had combined with the nephews of Khirâdhâro and conquered the country.

five months, and the prince and princess went on shore accompanied by the priests. An account is then given of the building of the temple, and the mode in which the relics were placed. The vessel now set sail for Dantapura, which it reached in little more than three months. The ambassadors of the king of Lankâ landed with the prince and princess. They were treated with much distinction, and remained in the country.

"After this follows a third tradition of a king, like the last named Dhammasoka,* who ruled the country of Arvadi, apparently Avanti (Ougein) with strict justice, but is forced by a famine to emigrate with his followers, amounting to 31,000 able-bodied men. The wanderers proceeded southward for seven months. After various adventures they reach a place where water and fish were abundant. Next day the king mounted his horse and reached the Diamond Sands. Here he meets the Nâga Râja, builds a Chaitya, and founds a city.

"Dhammasoka reigned here quietly for seven years, but mortified and unhappy because he could not reach the relics. His majesty accordingly offered a high reward to any one who should find the relics and disinhume them. But this proved of no avail. It so happened that, in the dilemma, a Putra of the king of Rom or Roum, named Kâkabhâsa, who happened to be trading to the country of Takkasila, encountered a violent storm. He had 500 souls on board, who, supplicating the gods, were rescued from death. The ship, with much difficulty, reached close to the Diamond Sands, and (the crew) observing signs of population, cast anchor with a view to refit.

"The Prince of Rom† assists the Nâga Râja to recover the hidden

---

* This is evidently a title, though, from the similarity of the name, Colonel Low confounds him with the great Asoka, and places him 321 B.C.

† It would be absurd to found any serious theory on the mention of the name of Rome, if it stood alone and unsupported. The circumstance mentioned in the narrative of the strangers being white men, and coming by sea, is a small confirmation that the people here mentioned were really Europeans. My impression, however, is, that few who are familiar with the arts of Rome in Constantine's time, and who will take the trouble to master these Amravati sculptures, can fail to perceive many points of affinity between them. The circular medallions of the arch of Constantine—such as belong to his time—and the general tone of the art of his age, so closely resemble what we find here, that the coincidence can hardly be accidental. The conviction that the study of these sculptures has forced on my mind is, that there was much more intercommunication between the East and the West during the period from Alexander to Justinian than is generally supposed, and that the intercourse was especially frequent and influential in the middle period, between Augustus and Constantine.

treasure, and to build a wonderful nine-storied Chaitya over it, many particulars of which are given; but as they are too long to extract, and either are imaginary or do not refer to the particular building we are engaged upon, it is hardly necessary to quote them here. These quotations might be multiplied to almost any extent; but enough has probably been adduced to show that, in the beginning of the fourth century—about the time when the struggle for the tooth-relic was convulsing all India—Buddhist tradition points most distinctly to the Diamond Sands, on the banks of the Kistnah, as the place where a great temple was being built. The kingdom of the Nâga Râja certainly was there; and so far as can be judged from every indication as to the locality, if it was not at or near Amravati, it could not possibly have been far from the spot.

"Though all this tends to confirm the idea that the building referred to is the Amravati Tope, the inference rises almost to certainty when we come to examine the sculptures with which it is adorned. In one bas-relief a ship is represented with two persons on board, bearing relics, and is being welcomed by a Nâga king on approaching the shore. In another an ark, in the form of a ship, like that described above, is being borne in state on men's shoulders; and in numerous scenes there are conferences between the Nâga king and a prince or king accompanied by a lady, neither of whom, nor any of whose suite, are Nâgas. Of course these scenes may represent other similar scenes which have happened to other people; but a careful examination of the whole presents so many points of coincidence that I hardly think they can be accidental. One point which the sculptures undoubtedly reveal is that Amravati was the capital, or, at least, residence of the Nâga Râja. In all the sculptures which do not relate to the life of Buddha, and in many of these, the Nâga king appears with his hood of a seven-headed snake, and all his women have also single snakes at the back of their heads. As will be presently shown, Nâga worship almost supersedes Buddhism in the religious representations, so much so, indeed, that it is sometimes difficult to say to which religion the temple is dedicated.

"It may be quite true that no single part of this evidence is sufficient to prove the case, but, taking the whole of it together, I think it must be admitted to be sufficient to justify the conclusion that the outer rails, at least, are part of the Temple at the Diamond Sands, which, according to the Ceylonese computation, was commenced in the year 322. Judging from its elaboration, it may have taken fifty years to complete. If this be so, the date of the completion may be about the year 370 or 380 of our era, and it may have remained complete for 150 or 200 years after that time, before it was deserted, as mentioned by Hiouen Thsang. That it was afterwards repaired and used for Buddhist purposes as late as the twelfth or thirteenth centuries seems also clear;* but the particulars of this restoration are less interesting, and further explorations on the spot are necessary before they can be made intelligible."

This account of the relic, though it gives the main features of the events recorded in the book now translated, is in some particulars different from that found in this Páli version, the substance of the information furnished by Mr Fergusson being derived also from sources other than the Sinhalese. The present work does not continue the history beyond the period of the arrival of the relic at Anurádhapura in Ceylon.

The tenth verse of the first chapter of Dá*t*hávansa shows that it was founded on an Elu or Sinhalese version of the history of the relic, and that the object which the Páli author had in view in his work was to make it more widely known in the East. At the end of the book is a brief notice of the author himself. His name was *Dhammakitti Thera;* and amongst his other titles to eminence, it appears, he was a "royal preceptor." We are informed that he was the author of many other books also, including amongst them a com-

* It is to be regretted that the Daladâwanso has not been completely translated, for it appears that in the twelfth or thirteenth century the tooth-relic was taken back to India at a time apparently when (1187) a Kírti Nissanga, a prince of Kalinga, was one of the many Indian princes who held sway in Ceylon. It is said to have been conveyed to the banks of the Ganges (Upham's History of Buddhism, p. 32), but, as Landresse suggests (Foĕ Kouĕ Ki, p. 345), this more probably was the Godavery, or, in other words, the Kistnah. From some particulars furnished me by Sir Walter Elliot, it seems that the part of the monument he dug into was a chapel formed of old slabs arranged unsymmetrically by some prince about that time, so as to form a chapel for some unexplained purpose. It may have been to receive this relic.

The inscription translated by Prinsep (J. A. S. B., vol. vi., p. 218) shows that Buddhism was flourishing at Amravati in—say the twelfth century. Altogether, nothing would surprise me less than to find that the tooth-relic sojourned here for seventy-six years before its recovery by the Ceylonese, about 1314 of our era. The materials exist for settling this question, but they have not yet been made available.

mentary on the Sanskrit Grammar of Chandragómi. He died during the reign of Queen Lílávatí, who commenced her reign in A.D. 1197, at Pollanaruva, or, as it is more correctly termed, Puluti Nagara, "city to the east" of Anurádhapura. Lílávatí herself was the queen of Parákkrama Báhu I., one of the most distinguished kings of Ceylon. It would seem that at this epoch there was an unusual activity displayed by the Sinhalese in the cultivation of not only the Elu and Páli, but also the Sanskrit.

It may be useful to add, that ample allusion is made to the tooth-relic in many other Páli and Sinhalese works, including the Mahawansa, especially in several chapters of the untranslated portions of it. From the native authorities, the relic appears to have migrated from place to place in Ceylon. Dislodged from Anurádhapura, when it first arrived from India, it has had its abode successively at Pollanaruva, Kacharagama, Pollanaruva again, Kotmalya, Beligala, Dambadania, Yápáruva, Kurunegala, Kottuwa, Situaka, Delgamuva, Nilembe, Hangurankete, Kondesale, and finally at Sirívardhanapura or Kandy.

To those who may be curious to know whether the relic now worshipped by the Buddhists in Ceylon is in truth the same which was brought over by Hemamálá and her husband from Dantapura, it may be necessary to state here that grave doubts have been thrown on its identity. Turnour writes: "Between A.D. 1303 and 1314, in the reign of Bhuwanekabáhu First, Ariyachchakkawati, the commander of an army sent by Kulesekera, king of Pandu, to invade Ceylon, got possession of the relic, and transferred it to Pandu. To treat for its recovery, the next monarch of the island, Parakkamo the Third, proceeded to Pandu in person, and was successful in his mission. According to Rebeiro it was captured by Constantine de Braganza during the wars of the Portuguese in 1560, and destroyed upon that occasion. The native authorities, however, represented that the relic was safely concealed at Delgamuva in Saffragam, during these wars. It was surrendered to the British, together with the Kandian kingdom in 1825." This extract, coupled with the notes already cited from Mr Fergusson's article on the subject, summarises nearly all that can be ascertained on this point. Those who have seen it think that it is of too great a size to be a human tooth, though this difficulty is sometimes met by fervent Buddhists with the exclamation, "True, but in Buddha's time, human beings were of much larger size than they are now!" Indeed, they may go further, and claim as a proof of identity the fact that the stains now observable in the relic were made the subject of remark centuries ago by King Pá*nd*u, as recorded in "Dá*t*hávansa."

In the preparation of this translation, and especially in the edition of the Páli text, much assistance has been derived by me from the accomplished Pandit Gunasekera, and the learned Buddhist priest Subhúti Unnánse of Vaska*d*uva. Several useful suggestions have also been furnished to me by that eminent Páli scholar Pandit Ba*t*uvantu*d*ava. Thanks are likewise due to the Government printer in Ceylon, Mr Herbert, for the pains he has bestowed on supervising the printing of the text.

It may not be irrelevant here to suggest, that fortunately there are at present to be found in the colony some Pandits, whose knowledge of Páli entitles them to take equal rank with such men as Rája Radhakant Deb or Vidyá Ságar, scholars so justly renowned for their proficiency in Sanskrit in Northern India. It is doubtful whether Ceylon is likely to produce hereafter amongst its native professors of Páli Pandits equally competent. It becomes, therefore, a matter of importance that no time should be lost by those who are interested in preventing the decay or corruption of Páli literature, in availing themselves of the services of such men in the editing whatever texts are procurable in the island. Indeed, some of the commentaries on

Páli works found in Ceylon are written in Sinhalese so ancient and abstruse that only by such men as these can they be utilised.

If, notwithstanding the labour bestowed by me on the preparation of this work, errors should have crept into the text or the translation, I must find consolation in what one of my countrymen, Sri Vijayarakshita, a Hindu poet, has so truly said—

> "Martyair asarvavidurair vihite kva náma
> Granthe 'sti doshavirahah suchirantane 'pi?"

"In what work done by non-omniscient mortals, even though it be of long-standing, is there the absence of faults?"

NOTE.

☞ [It is necessary to state here, to prevent any confusion of ideas that may arise in the mind of the general reader, that the poet, in order to avoid tautology, employs a large variety of names to designate Buddha—such as the Teacher, the Lord of the three worlds, the King of sages, Tathágata, Sugata, the Conqueror, the Sage, the King or Lord of the Law, Him possessed of the ten powers, the Five-eyed one, the Chief of men,* &c. To the student of Oriental languages, however, the context alone ought to be an ample guide in this respect.]

* This last expression is also used to designate some of the kings whose names occur in this book.

THE DÁTHÁVANSA;

OR,

THE HISTORY OF THE TOOTH-RELIC.

ADORATION TO HIM, THE BLESSED, THE SANCTIFIED, THE ALL-WISE.

CHAPTER I.

1

I worship the Teacher,[1] who is wise, avoids the path of heresy, is the lamp of the three worlds,[2] endures the unendurable, removes all obstacles to knowledge, (and) whose sphere of understanding is infinite.

2

I worship the Law,[3] which emanates from the Lord of the three worlds, removes fear, is observed by those (established) in the very pure Vijjá[4] and Chara*n*a,[5] severs the bonds of Papancha[6] and Saññojana,[7] is subtle, (and) difficult of comprehension.

3

I worship the Association,[8] (which consists of) the disciples of the King of sages, who are worthy of offerings, and have their senses under complete control, by merely bearing good-will towards whom souls attain the sorrow-destroying, deathless[9] state.

4

Parakkama, an ornament to the race of Ká*l*aka Nágara,[10] a merciful commander of the army, a seeker of the welfare of the religion of Buddha, having the prosperity of the people at heart,

5, 6[11]

Placed in royal power over all Lanká,[12] Queen Lílávatí,[13] who—born of the race, spotless as the moon, of Pa*nd*u,[14] having faith in the religion of the King of sages awakened (in her), sweet-worded, following the path of justice, being always unto her subjects like a mother who brought them forth, possessed of high intelligence, giving[15] whatever was asked of her—was the beloved wife of King Parakkama Báhu ;[16]

7

Made the pious prince, Madhurinda by name—who had good ministers whom he propitiated, was very compassionate, born of the race of Pa*nd*u kings—thoroughly instructed in the word of Buddha and in the Arts ;[17]

8

Removed the widely-known disgrace that the threefold Síhala[18] had for a very considerable time no king, and long pleased the priests, who had their senses well restrained, with excellent robes and the like.[19]

9

Being respectfully requested by him (Parakkama), who wished for the long endurance of Buddha's word, was grateful, endowed with valour and wisdom, possessed of a good memory, and renowned like the moon,[20]

10

I render into the Mágadhí[21] language, for the benefit of those who live in other islands also,[22] the history of the tooth-relic of Buddha, recounted in the language of their own country by the poets of Síhala.

11

Once upon a time, the Conqueror[23] having become (incarnate) as a young man, Sumedha by name, skilled in researches in the Vedas and Vedangas,[24] in a wealthy Brahman family, in the prosperous city called Amara,[25]

12

Thought within himself—" Suffering from the misfortune of repeated births,[26] overcome by old age, overwhelmed by death, I should seek the happy state which is free from birth, decay, and the like,"

13

(And), bestowing on the poor possessions of wealth and corn in large quantities, not easy to be parted with, abandoned many friends, children and relations, who had followed him through excessive affection,

14

(And), casting away all sensuous pleasures delightful to the mind, left his home,[27] proceeded to a mountain near the Himáchala,[28] known by the name Dhammika, adorned by many rows of trees,

15

(And) assumed the guise of a hermit, being clothed with the bark of a tree, bearing the hide of the antelope, wearing matted hair, in a hermitage pleasing to the mind, inaccessible to evil beasts, erected by the king of gods.[29]

16

This hermit, his mind well controlled, his senses destroyed, maintaining his frame with fruits of different kinds, reached the farthest point in transcendent knowledge,[30] (and) enjoyed there the happiness resulting from meditation.[31]

17, 18

Whilst his own part of the road was incomplete, the hermit Sumedha saw Dípankara Buddha[32]—to whom the farthest shore of the fathomless sea of knowable things was perceptible, who had reached the end of repeated births, was void of desire, had no superior, going, once upon a time, attended by many tens of thousands of saints[33]—on a road thoroughly made by the great mass of people who lived in the city, Ramma,[34] exulting at the expected arrival of Buddha.

19

Then devoting his body and life to the Lord of the three

worlds and the Association, he spread his matted hair, the hide and the like, (and) made his body itself a bridge over the pit of mud;

20

Having reflected—"Let Him of great mercy, with the priests, go over (my) back, without treading on the mud," (and) perceived that these three worlds were in a helpless state, he lay down there.

21

He, whose heart was moved by compassion, (being also endowed) with superior strength of mind, made a great resolution to attain Buddhahood, in order to rescue from the sea of existence the beings suffering from sorrow.

22

Conscious then of the aspiration of the hermit, the great Sage gave an assurance (of his becoming Buddha at a future time); afterwards on Tathágata[35] going into the city, the hermit by himself reflected on the Páramí virtues.[36]

23

And then, possessed of unflinching courage, he completed the practising of the many holy virtues required for the maturing of Buddhahood, in different births, during four Asankheyyas[37] and ten thousand Kappas.[38].

24

Then he, greatly renowned, born in the Tusíta[39] world, looking to the time of his attainment of holy Buddhahood, having for his wealth[40] compassion, long enjoyed happiness in every respect.

25

Respectfully requested to attain Buddhahood by many Chiefs of gods[41] and other beings, who, elated with joy, came from ten thousand Chakkaválas,[42]

26

The ever intelligent One, leaving then (the Tusita heavens), became the son of King Suddhodana,[43] the matchless chief[44] of the Sakya race,[45] by his queen Mahámáyá, in the city called Kapila.[46]

27

As soon as he was born, he stood on the earth, (and) looked towards the (different) quarters; then they opened out (like) courtyards, and gods and men worshipped him there.

28

The gods invisible in the skies held umbrellas and the like, and he, proceeding seven steps, looking towards the north, uttered a fearless expression.[47]

29

He, who was rightly called Siddhattha Kumára,[48] of much strength, endowed with a body pleasing from its youthfulness, enjoyed happiness in three magnificent palaces, suited to the three seasons.

30

Observing one day on the road to the park a man overcome by old age, also a sick man, a dead man, and a mendicant, in succession, his mind disgusted with repeated births, he longed to become an ascetic.

31

Then he, who was very merciful, attended by the denizens of heaven bearing in their hands flowers, lamps, and other things, departed during the night, accompanied by Channaka,[49] (and) conveyed by his horse Kanthaka.

32

Having in due course reached the river Anoma,[50] he stood on the sandbank, pleasing as well-cleansed pearl, (and) threw towards the sky his tuft of beautiful hair, cut off with a sharp sword,

33

The Chief of the gods receiving it then in a casket of pure gold, built (for it) in his city a Chúláma*n*i[51] monument of blue gems, of three yójanas[52] (in height).

34

Then he (Siddattha) wore the yellow robe and other necessaries, brought by the Brahma Ghaṭikára;[53] afterwards assuming a form, praised (by the gods), he threw his two garments towards the sky.

35

Brahma, of great power, influenced by the weight of his piety, received them, and erected (for it) in his world a cloth-monument[54] of blue gems and other precious stones, of twelve yójanas (in height).

36

Having a well-regulated mind, possessed of good memory, his senses subdued, of a modest demeanour, freed from the desire for flavoured (food), highly courageous, he exercised for six years together difficult (and) great perseverance.[55]

37

And on the day of the full moon[56] in the month of May, going near the foot of the Bodhi-tree,[57]—which came into existence (simultaneously) with him—resolving to be courageous, he sat on a grass seat, measuring fourteen cubits.

38

At nightfall, the Conqueror, making the earth and its mountains tremble, vanquished the army of Mára,[58] which overspread the earth and the heavens, causing terror by the hideous forms which it assumed.

39

The three worlds being decorated by multitudes of gods, Asuras,[59] and Brahmas, with festoons of flowers and the like, the sound of divine kettle-drums resounding, he attained Buddhahood at the close of the night.

40

Then the ten thousand systems of worlds, with their rocks and forests, quaked, the salt sea became sweet, great light spread through the worlds;

41

The blind received clear eyesight; even those who from birth were deaf heard sounds; the dumb conversed in pleasing speech; the lame walked gracefully on their feet;

42

The hunchbacked had straight and pleasing bodies; even the fire in the lowest and other hells[60] was extinguished; living beings were released from their bonds; hunger and other sensuous appetites disappeared from the world of Petas;[61]

43

The diseases and sufferings of living beings were alleviated; fear oppressed not irrational animals; men were gifted with smooth and pleasant speech; elephants trumpeted,

44

And horses neighed with a cheerful air; all (kinds of) drums resounded of themselves; the bodily ornaments[62] of living beings made a noise; all the (different) quarters were clear throughout;

45

A gentle, refreshing, and cool breeze blew; clouds showered rain out of season; birds abandoned their movements in the skies; water welled out, cleaving the earth;

46

Rivers stood still, as if not flowing; all the stars shone intensely in the firmament; the worlds on every side were open to view; there was neither death nor birth to men;

47

Mountains and the like formed no hindrance to beholders; a scent coveted by even the gods pervaded; trees bore fruits and flowers; the sea was covered with lotuses;

48

Various flowers which blossom on land and water expanded in full; the whole space between the earth and sky was filled, without a void, by a shower of flowers and scents.

49

Then Buddha spent seven days, sitting on that splendid seat, enjoying the long-wished-for happiness resulting from the exercise of meditation.

50

Afterwards the great Sage, ascending to the vault of the skies, (and) exhibiting a double miracle,[63] removed the doubts of the denizens of heaven about his Buddhahood.

51

Then descending, he stood near the north-east corner of the seat of Victory,[64] (and) worshipped, with unclosed eye, for seven days that seat and the Bodhi-tree.

52

Thereupon Buddha walked for seven days together in a gem-court of great value, made by the eminent gods, in the space (intervening) between the seat and the place where he stood.

53

Afterwards Buddha spent seven days together seated in the hall of gems, in the western direction of the Bodhi-tree, meditating on the rules of the Samanta Paṭṭhána.[65]

54

Then a multitude of rays proceeding from the body of Buddha, meeting no obstacle, spread on all sides, above and below, in the immeasurable worlds.

55

He who is without a superior, (and) has infinite powers of perception, served by the king of gods, lived for seven days at the root of the banyan-tree called Ajapála,[66] enjoying the happiness resulting from meditation.

56

Buddha passed seven days in meditation, at the root of the

tree Muchalinda,[67] seated in a temple made of the coils of the snake Muchalinda, with flowers scattered over it.

57

The Sage passed seven nights and days, in a state of meditation, at the tree Rájáyatana;[68] then the thousand-eyed god furnished the Teacher with a tooth-cleanser and water to wash his face.

58

Converting into one the four bowls of stone brought by the eminent guardian deities, he received therein powdered grain (and) balls of sweetmeats mixed with honey, brought by (some) merchants.

59

Having finished his meal, (and) confirmed the two (merchants), Tapassu and Bhalluka[69] in the Saranas, he stroked his head, (and) gave them (some) hair, in order that they might worship it.

60

Requested by the great Sahampati,[70] at the root of the banyan-tree called Ajapála, the Sage went alone to Báránasí,[71] to secure to the people the advantage derived from his excellent doctrine.

61

The King of the Law, having gone to the grove Isipatana,[72] the abode of ascetics, (and) sitting on a couch there provided for (him) in the unvarying place, in July, on the full-moon day—the world being illumined by the rays of the moon—caused to prevail the dominion of the Law[73] which removes the sinful impurities of gods, Brahmas, and others.

62

One hundred and eighty millions of Brahmas, with the Brahman sage named Añña Ko*nd*añña[74] at their head, having heard that most excellent Law, which filled the entire space of the three worlds, comprehended the doctrine of the Paths.[75] Instantaneously a great light appeared in the illimitable worlds, and there were many kinds of miracles.

CHAPTER II.

1–3

The Teacher, from that time instructing gods and men, came to Lanká in the month Phussa,[1] the ninth from (the attainment of) Buddhahood, at full moon, and proceeded to the assembly of Yakkhas[2] in the park Mahánágavana,[3] one yójana in breadth, three yójanas in length, (situated) at the bank of a river, (and) standing there in the sky, afflicted the Yakkhas with fear caused by wind, darkness, (and) rain.

4, 5

Spreading a piece of hide on the ground presented by those Yakkhas who received assurances of protection, he sat, (and) extended at that instant, by supernatural power, (that) piece of hide, which abounded with rows of flames of fire burning on all sides, as far as the sea;

6

(And) bringing over hither Giridípa,[4] he established there the Yakkhas, who quickly assembled on the sea-shore.

7

Then Buddha, having preached the Law at the assembly of the gods, made many ko*t*ís[5] of beings to comprehend the truth.

8

The Conqueror, having given his hair to god Mahásumana[6] on Mount Sumanakú*t*a,[7] to worship it, went to Jetavana.[8]

9

He (Mahásumana), placing the hair on the ground, (which formed) the seat whereon the Teacher sat, (and) erecting (for it) a Thúpa[9] of emerald, worshipped it.

10

Finding the Nágas[10] Chúlodara and Mahodara, living on mountain and sea, anxious to fight for the sake of a gem-couch,

11

The great Sage came to Nágadípa,[11] on a holy day, in the fifth year from his Buddhahood, in the month of April, in the dark half of the lunar month.

12, 13

Then the god Samiddhi Sumana, having removed the tree Rájáyatana which stood at Jetavana—as his abode, resembling a mountain of emerald—(and) holding it (as) an umbrella for the Teacher, came with him pleased in mind.

14

A great war prevailing between the two Nága kings, the Lord, seated in the sky, produced intense darkness.

15

Then, having caused light to be seen, (and) comforted the Nágas, the Chief of men preached the Law of reconciliation.

16

Eighty ko*t*ís of Nágas, living on mountain and sea, being pleased, were established in the Sílas and Chara*n*as.[12]

17

Presenting the gem-couch to the Teacher, the Nága kings satisfied the mighty hero seated there with food and drink.

18

Planting there the tree Rájáyatana, he gave it and the couch to the Nágas for worshipping them.

19

Invited by the Nága chief, called Ma*n*iakkhika, in the eighth year from Buddhahood, in May, at full moon,

20

He came, with five hundred priests, to the well-built mansion of the self-same Nága king, at Kalyá*n*í.[13]

21

The Chief of men sat on a costly seat in the gem-hall, built at the site of the Thúpa, at Kalyá*n*í.

22

Then the Nága chief, attended by the Nágas, satisfied the Chief of the world and the priests with divine food of various kinds.

23

The Teacher having preached the good Law, which confers the happiness of heaven and Nibbána, stamped his footprint[14] on Sumanakú*t*a.

24

Then the Chief and the priests, having rested during the day at the foot of the mountain, went to Díghavápi.[15]

25

Buddha and the priests seated there, at the site of the Thúpa, enjoyed the incomparable happiness derived from meditation.[16]

26

The Conqueror entered into meditation at the site of the great Bodhi-tree, and was also in (the exercise of) meditation, at the site of the Maháthúpa.

27

Buddha, the perfect, spent a while in the enjoyment of meditation at the site of the Thúpa, in Thúpáráma,[17] with the assembly of priests.

28

The Sage, who knows the (three) times,[18] standing at the site of the Siláthúpa,[19] instructed the gods thoroughly, and went thereafter to Jetavana.

29

Not caring for gain or acts of hospitality,[20] enduring unendurable insults, desiring only the deliverance of all worlds;

30

Having lived forty and five years, (and) preached the religion of the Teacher, consisting of nine parts,[21] such as Sutta and the like;

31

Having caused persons beyond number to cross the desert of existence, (and) fulfilled all the duties of a Buddha;

32

In the city Kusinárá,[22] at the grove of Sála[23]-trees, Upavattana, belonging to the Malla kings,[24] in the space intervening between two Sála-trees;

33

Reclining on a couch of great value, well set up, with his head to the north, in the sleeping attitude of a lion, in May, at full moon;

34

The (five)-eyed one[25] * preached to the Mallas his excellent Law, at the first watch[26] of the night, (and) caused Subhadda to attain the state of Nibbána at the middle watch.

35

And having included in the word Appamáda[27] all sections of the Law, he exhorted the priests at the last watch of the night.

36

At the time of dawn, having risen from the exercise of reflection and meditation,[28] he attained Nibbána, being freed from (all) remains of attachment.

37

There were then earthquakes and other portents, causing astonishment; there were (also) many kinds of offerings made by gods and men.

* *Vide* v. 31.

38

From what is stated in order at the end of Parinibbána[29] Sutta, the peculiarity of (these) offerings can be fully ascertained by those who desire it.

39

Having first wrapped Buddha with new cloth, (and) wrapped him then with clean cotton-wool also;

40

Having thus carefully wrapped him over five hundred times, and placed him in a golden coffin filled with oil,[30]

41

The chiefs of the Mallas placed him then on a funeral pile[31] made of scented wood, one hundred and twenty cubits in height.

42

Owing to the will of the gods, that "so long as the king of the Law was not worshipped by the priest Máha Kassapa[32] the funeral pile should not take fire,"

43

The chiefs of the Malla princes, though exerting themselves in various ways, were unable to make that funeral pile burn.

44, 45

The feet of Buddha, which by the wish of the priest Máhá Kassapa came out, dividing into two the cloth and the great trough and pile of great value, lay on his (the priest's) head; having been worshipped (by him) they lay again where they were before.

46

Thereafter, by the power of the gods, fire was kindled in the pile; there was neither soot nor ashes of the body of the Teacher when burnt.

47

By the will of Buddha there remained relics of the colour

of pearls and of the lustre of gold scattered in various ways.

48

These seven relics, the bone of the forehead, the two collar-bones, (and) the four tooth-relics of Buddha were not dispersed.

49

Streams of water descending from the skies, and rising from the earth on all sides, extinguished the fire of the pile.

50

The priest named Sarabhú, the disciple of the priest Sáriputta, who was endowed with supernatural power, (and) had attained the fourfold knowledge,[33]

51

Having removed the neck-relic from the funeral pile, placed it in the Thúpa at Mahiyangana,[34] (and) made a monument encasing it.

52

The Sage called Khema, possessed of kindness, (and) freed from Saññójana,[35] took then the left tooth-relic from the funeral pile.

53

Then the eminent Brahman Do*n*a,[36] appeasing the quarrel which rose amongst eight kings on account of the relics of Buddha,

54

(And) dividing the remaining relics, made them into eight portions, (and) gave them to eight kings living in different cities.

55

The kings, exceedingly joyful, received those relics, (and) departing, built monuments (for them), each in his own country.

56

One relic was honoured and worshipped by Sakka,[37] one by the inhabitants of Gandhára,[38] one by the Nága kings.

57

Then Khema gave the tooth-relic taken by him to Brahmadatta, king of Kalinga,[39] in Dantapura.

58

Having extinguished all scepticism by preaching the Law, he made that king pleased with the excellent three gems.[40]

59

The king, plunging into the great sea of nectar of the Law of the eminent Sage, washed off his stains—avarice, and the like.

60

The best of men, as if he were a rain-cloud, allayed the heat of poverty by showers of various gems.

61–63

The king caused to be made for the tooth-relic a temple inlaid with gold, adorned with hanging pearl-necklaces, abounding in hundreds of rooms at the top, difficult, like the early sun, to look at, owing to the radiance of various gems dazzling the eyes—a vehicle to heaven and to Nibbána, which produces excessive delight; he also made for the relic, in the same place, a seat resplendent with gems.

64

Placing there the tooth-relic of the great Sage, he honoured it unweariedly, night and day, with the requisites of worship.[41]

65

Having in this manner amassed heaps of the wealth of merit, he left his human frame, (and) adorned the heavenly assembly.[42]

66

Then his son called Kasírája, born after his likeness, accepting the kingdom, removed the dart of sorrow from the ministers.

67

Worshipping the tooth-relic with flowers, scents, and other necessaries, he constantly illuminated the relic-temple with gem-lamps.

68

That king, having acquired a heap of merit in this and other manners, abandoned his (human) body, and went to the city of the Chief of the gods.

69

Then there was his son, a great king, Sunanda by name, who delighted good men, and took a personal interest in the religion of Buddha.

70

Having revered with great exercise of piety the tooth-relic of Him who sees the end of things worthy of knowing, he went to be associated with the gods.

71

And afterwards many other kings also, in succession, worshipped the tooth-relic of the supreme Sage.

72

Then a king called Guhasíva, whose commands were inviolable, having attained the royal state, conferred benefits on the people.

73

Not discriminating between his own interests and those of others, he did acts of kindness to the Niga*n*thas,[43] who were greedy of gain and adoration, artful, (and) blind through ignorance.

74

The chief of men, enveloped in a mass of ignorance, like the moon at the time of rain, was unable to shine with the rays of virtue.

75

When digressing from the path of truth, he strayed into

the wilderness of heresy, other people (however) transgressed not the good path.

76

The citizens, decorating the city with rows of golden triumphal arches,[44] flags, plantain-trees, and numerous festoons of flowers,

77

With sounds of festal praise, dancing, singing, and other amusements; with flowers of gold (and) silver; with scented powder and the like,

78

Worshipped the tooth-relic of the supreme Sage, (and) made at times (the city to be) of one continued noise, as if it were the sea raging at the destruction of the world.[45]

79

The king, drawing up a window[46] in the palace, (and) looking out, saw the people engaged in performing the rites of worship.

80

Then the king, astonished, was filled with curiosity, (and) uttered this word in the midst of the assembly of ministers:—

81

"What wonder (is) this? what sort of a miracle? (Why is it that) this city of mine should be engaged in festive rejoicings?"

82

Then an intelligent minister, who took a personal interest in Buddha, said to the king ignorant of the power of Buddha:—

83

"O great king! this relic of Buddha, who found the (means of) extinguishing desire, (and) who subdues all, was brought (hither) by the priest Khema.

84

"Former kings here, having associated with virtuous

friends and worshipped this relic, went to the heavenly world.

85

"All these citizens too, eager for happiness in the next world, having assembled together, are worshipping the relic of Buddha."

86

The king, hearing the well-spoken religious discourse of the minister, renounced the filth of heresy, (and) became a convert to the threefold gem.

87

The king, rendering to the relic a worship which caused astonishment, made the heretics distressed and other people pleased.

88, 89

Thinking thus:—"All these are shameless, destitute of piety and other virtues, hard-hearted, hypocritical, unwise, obstacles to heaven and Nibbána," King Guhasíva expelled all those Nig*an*thas from his country.

90

Then all the Nig*an*thas, inflamed by the heat of anger, like fires with clarified butter sprinkled (over them), went to the city of Pá*t*aliputta.[47]

91

At that time there was a king of great glory named Pa*nd*u, Lord of Jambudípa,[48] possessed of innumerable forces and vehicles.

92

Now, all those Nig*an*thas, blind through anger, uttering slander, approached the king, and said this word:—

93

"Thou constantly worshippest the gods Siva,[49] Brahma, and the like, who are possessed of extraordinary power, and are worthy of being adored by all gods and men.

94

"But thy neighbour, king Guhasíva, reviling such gods, is now worshipping the bone of a dead body."[50]

95

Then the king, hearing their speech, brought under the influence of anger, addressed Chittayána, a valiant and a tributary king, (thus):—

96

"Go to the Kalinga country; bring here Guhasíva and the bone of the dead body worshipped by him night and day."

97

Then King Chittayána, having prepared his great fourfold army,[51] started from the city.

98

The king having proceeded, at the head of his forces, encamped at no great distance from Dantapura.

99

The king of Kalinga, having heard of his arrival, pleased that chief of men with gifts of noble elephants and the like.

100

Chittayána, having observed that King Guhasíva entertained good intentions, entered Dantapura with (his army).

101

That king saw the city teeming with walls, gates, towers, palaces, festoon-works, and abounding in almsgiving halls.[52]

102

Then the king, going with a glad heart, entered the palace, (and) communicated to Guhasíva the message of King Pa*nd*u.

103

Listening to his terrific and inviolable message, he (Guhasíva), with a bright colour on his face, addressed Chittayána:—

104

"Having during many Kappas unweariedly fulfilled the duties required for the attainment of Buddhahood, by the gift of his flesh, eyes, and other things, for the benefit of the whole world;

105

"And, vanquishing the army of Mára, attaining the extinction of all passions, (and), through unobstructed knowledge, arriving at the furthest shore of all truths;

106

"And disregarding the enjoyment of happiness during this life, he rescued the entire mass of beings from the sea of (repeated) existence, by the aid of his ship, the Law;

107

"That man is indeed deceived who despises Buddha, the God of gods, the refuge of all beings."

108

The king, hearing this and similar praise of the Teacher, made manifest his happiness by a continuous flow of tears of joy.

109

Guhasíva, observing that Chittayána was pleased, went with him into the relic-temple of great value.

110–112

He saw the relic-temple—resplendent with door-posts and the like, made of the sandal-wood of Mount Hari,[53] with rows (of images) in coral, of tigers with pendant pearl-strings, with emerald windows, with tinkling bells of gems, with golden (suspended) garlands at its angles; having a spire of gems, (and) a roof lofty and shining with lapis lazuli; abounding in paintings of sea-monsters[54]—(and) a seat radiant with gems for the relic.

113

Then, beholding the relic-shrine glittering with gems under a white umbrella, he was pleased and astonished.

114

Then the lord of Kalinga, opening the shrine, pressed his right knee-orb on the earth;

115

(And) calling to mind the virtues, the tenfold power[55] and the like, of the supreme Buddha, he prayed, with the palms of his hands clasped together and uplifted :—

116

" All beings were pleased by thee, who didst exhibit at the root of the tree Ga*nd*amba[56] a double and stupendous miracle for subduing the heretics,

117

" Making the surface of the world filled with water and fire proceeding from the fore and other parts of thy body.

118

" (Also) descending from Távatinsa to the city Sankassa, after preaching for three months Abhidhamma[57] to the gods;

119

" Worshipped in various ways by Brahmas, gods, Asuras, and the like, who held in their hands umbrellas, chámaras,[58] conches, and other things;

120

" A miracle called Lokavivara*n*a[59] was exhibited by thee, standing on a stair of gems created by Vissakamma;[60]

121

" O supreme Sage! in like manner in numerous places again many miracles were exhibited by thee, the Self-existent.

122

"To-day also a miracle, conferring the happiness of heaven and Nibbána on the men who are (here) looking on, should be shown by thee."

123

The tooth-relic, beautiful as the digit of the moon, ascending the vault of the sky,—shooting forth silver-white rays, emitting rapidly smoke, flickering many a time, extinguishing (again) the flame for a while,—performed a miracle pleasing to the eye.

124

King Chittayána, having witnessed that very pleasing miracle, was delighted, (and) renouncing the net of heresy to which he had been long accustomed, attained, with all the divisions of his army, incomparable refuge in Buddha, (and) acquired pre-eminent merit by highly honouring the relic in various ways.

CHAPTER III.

1

Afterwards the valiant Chittayána, greatly pleased, made known to the king of Kalinga that the order of King Pa*nd*u was inviolable.

2

The king then adorning the city Dantapura—which had the numerous rays of the sun (pouring on it) screened off by great canopies—with flags, flowers, incense, and triumphal arches;

3

Attended by the inhabitants of market-towns[1] and cities, who had their eyes suffused by a flow of tears; carrying on his own head the relic-casket of great value,

4

Mounted a chariot having a large and white umbrella raised over it, yoked to horses—white as the interior of the conch-shell, (and) of a colour like that of the early sun—(and rendered) lovely by a carpet of diverse colours;

5

(And) accompanied by a large number of his troops, resembling the sea that overflows the shore, (and) followed by the minds, though not by the bodies,[2] of many people,

6

Came to a long and broad road, which—all its sides being well spread over with sand, well decorated with vases filled (with scented water)[3] and the like, strewn with flowers—led to Pá*t*aliputta.

7

The king of Kalinga, in company with the gods of the

woods, worshipped daily the tooth-relic on the road with flowers and other requisites, with dancing, singing, and instrumental music.[4]

8

The lord of men, carrying the relic, came by degrees to the end of the road, which was difficult to traverse owing to rivers and mountains, and entered the city called Pá*t*aliputta.

9

Then the king of kings, noticing that the king (of Kalinga) was fearless and unapprehensive in the midst of the assembly, overcome by anger, addressed the slandering Niga*nt*has (thus) :—

10

"Throw now into a burning heap of charcoal the bone worshipped by this man, who had abandoned the gods worthy of adoration, (and) burn it without delay."

11

Then the Niga*nt*has, pleased in mind, prepared at the royal courtyard a coal-pit, large, deep, and full of heaps of coals (burning) without a flame.

12

Thereupon the heretics, blind through ignorance, threw the tooth-relic into that (pit) burning intensely on all sides, bright and horrid as the (hell) Roruva.[5]

13

By its influence, bursting through the heap of fire, there arose a lotus of the size of a chariot-wheel, with a quantity of pollen rising on all sides, and lovely from the weight of its filaments.

14

At that moment the tooth-relic of Buddha, resting on the pericarp of the lotus, illumined all directions with brilliant rays white as the kunda flower.[6]

15

The men, witnessing this wonder, pleased in mind, worshipped the tooth-relic of Buddha with gems and the like, (and) renounced each his own heresy.

16

But King Pa*n*d*u, not renouncing the net of heresy in which he had been long bound, placed the tooth-relic on an anvil (and) caused it to be struck with a sledge-hammer.

17

The (relic), sinking into the anvil, with only one half visible, illumined all directions with its rays, like the moon standing on the eastern mountain.

18

Witnessing the power of the tooth-relic of Buddha, that chief king became astounded. A Niga*nt*ha then, moved by envy, said this to the king of kings :—

19

"O king! there were in the world various incarnations of Janaddana,[7] such as Ráma[8] and the like ; this bone is a part of him. If not, whence such influence as this?"

20

"If the saying is true, that it is certainly a part of the body, left behind, of that god, who, born man, went afterwards to heaven for the benefit (of mankind),

21

"Celebrating the many virtues of Náráyana,[9] possessed of great power, remove, whilst I look on, this (relic) sunk in the anvil here,

22

"And, making the faces of the great multitude beautiful as the lotus, receive such kind of wealth as you desire ;" thus said the king to the garrulous Niga*nt*has.

23

Those hypocritical heretics, praising highly the god Vishnu, by (dwelling upon) his attributes of various kinds, sprinkled the relic with water.[10] It nevertheless moved not from the place where it lay.

24

Then the chief of the earth, despising the Niganthas, and searching for the means of dislodging the relic, made a proclamation in his city by beat of drums :—

25

"Whoever removes to-day the relic buried in the anvil here shall attain prosperity, receiving much wealth in the presence of the king."

26

Hearing this important proclamation made by beat of drum, a bold scion of the nobility in that city, Subhadda (by name), desirous of acquiring merit, and pleased with the power of Buddha, entered the king's assembly.

27

Having then made obeisance to that chief king, he, with a mind freed from fear, depicted the splendour of the virtues of the Omniscient[11] in language going to the hearts of those congregated (there) :—

28, 29

"That Anáthapi*nd*appada,[12] the chief of nobles, who, purchasing a land for immense wealth, caused to be built (thereon) a monastery called Jetavana,[13] pleasing to the mind, and, dedicating it to Buddha, waited upon him with the four requisites,[14] was (even) my great-grandfather, who had found the path to Nibbána. Witness ye now the weight of my (own) piety towards the Lord of the three worlds, the King of the Law."

30

He, possessed of much wisdom, having thus spoken, throwing his outer upper garment on one of his shoulders, (and) touching the surface of the earth with the right knee, said, with clasped hands :—

31

"Of that Tathágata[15] * who, being once an elephant of the Chaddanta tribe, though, from being shot by a poisoned arrow, he had his body smeared with blood, (yet) cut off his tusks, lustrous with six coloured rays, (and) gave them to the hunter (who pursued him);

32

"Who, again, as a hare, of a pure nature, anxious to give his own self away, roasted his body in a heap of burning coals, and presented it to a hungry Brahman;

33

"Who, again, being the eminent king Sivi, as if not satisfied with giving away things exterior to himself, presented also his bright eyes to an old (and) blind Brahman, for the sake of (attaining) Buddhahood;

34

"Who, again, being Khantivádin (the hermit), even when King Kalábu caused his feet and hands to be cut off, (and) his body was (then) drenched in blood, endured (the sufferings, and) was friendly to him, as towards one who had conferred glory on him;

35

"Who, again, as Dhammapála, did not permit his mind to be ill-disposed, even though his own wicked father, King Patápa, caused the (punishment of) Asimálakamma to be inflicted (on him) when he was but seven months old;

36

"Who, again, as a monkey, though his own forehead was broken with a stone by a wicked man rescued (by himself) from a precipice in the forest, yet guided him who did not know (his path in the forest) to a safe place;

* *Vide* v. 52.

37

"Who, moreover, as a nobleman, stood on a great lotus-flower, which rose instantly, dividing a burning pit of charcoal created by the enraged Mára, (and) gave alms;

38

"By whom, again, as a deer that had placed its own head on the block to save from death a doe which was about to be delivered (of its young one, and) was in a state of fear, other multitudes of living beings also were saved;

39

"Who, again, as Sambhava by name, when only in his seventh year, fond of playing in the sand in the streets, being requested by Suchírata, explained an intricate question after the manner of the Omniscient;

40

"Who, again, as the chief of monkeys, gave up the attachment even to his own life, wound round his belly a ratan-creeper, (and) delivered many thousands of monkeys from death;

41

"Who, again, as the hog Tu*nd*ila, satisfied the people with the taste of the nectar of the Law, and as a sage, composing a treatise on logic, made his own Law prevail for a long time;

42

"Who, as Vidhura by name, possessed of a keen intellect, subdued, on the summit of Ká*l*agiri, the devil Pu*nn*aka, a cruel foe, endowed with great supernatural powers, and addicted to sensuous appetites.

43

"Who, again, as a young quail, (though) remaining unfledged in the nest, (yet) being wise, quenched by the power of truth, as a cloud (abates it) by rain, a fiercely burning forest fire;

44

"Who, again, as the king of fishes, finding the fishes thirsty and fainting at a time when there was no rain, made in an instant the country overrun with heavy floods by the word of truth;

45

"Who, again, in his birth as Vessantara, made gifts of elephants, horses, chariots, and the like, which were decorated in various ways, and caused the earth to quake, (also) children born after his likeness, and wives of equal (rank and beauty);

46

"Who, again, becoming Buddha, not caring for the happiness of this life, practising kindness, enduring all (kinds of) ridicule and the like, did good, difficult of performance, to the world;

47

"Who, again, conquered the devil Álavaka, rushing with a very formidable (and) powerful army, armed with an invincible weapon, (and) possessed of great supernatural powers;

48

"Who, again, as an eminent sage, making the Brahma world distressed by a series of flames of fire proceeding from his body, crushed the heresy which had long prevailed there, (and) brought to submission a noble Brahma;

49

"Who, again, conquered the elephant Dhanapála, which, being beyond (the control of) the hook, his temples being drenched with ichor, ran forward like the horrible Mára, making towers, gates, and the like, to fall;

50

"Who, as a being of great mercy, vanquished the robber Angulimála, who had his hands and feet red with the blood of men, and chased him, waving a sword difficult to be encountered by others;

51

"Who, as the King of the Law, conquering hosts of enemies, caused the dominion of his excellent Law to prevail, and enabled all his followers to plunge into the ocean of good doctrine.

52

"Of that Tathágata, the supreme chief of sound doctrine, who has no rival, is infinitely wise, endowed with the four-fold knowledge, and possessed of great mercy, this is the relic.

53

"By this truth, let the relic of Buddha ascend instantly to the vault of the skies, (and) shining like the digit of the moon, dispel the doubts of the masses of the people."

54

At that moment the tooth-relic of Buddha, ascending to the skies, (and) illumining all directions, like the planet Venus,[16] pleased the people, their doubts being removed.

55

Then the (relic), descending from the courtyard of the skies, placed itself on the head of the son of nobles, (and) gratified that man borne down with piety, as if he had his body saturated with nectar.

56

The Niga*n*thas, having witnessed this miracle, said to King Pa*nd*u as follows:—"O king! this is the magical power[17] of the son of the nobles; it is not the influence of the relic."

57

The king, hearing their word, addressed Subhadda, the son of the nobles, thus:—"Show another miracle of this nature, in order that these (men) may be convinced."

58

Then Subhadda, remembering the wonderful deeds of the

supreme Sage, placed the relic in a golden bowl filled with scented and cool water.

59

The (relic), moving swiftly, as if it were a royal swan, in the scented water, with its right side turned (towards the spectators), rising and sinking, made the people bearers of tears of joy.

60

And then having made a pit in the middle of the street, he threw the relic therein, filled it well with earth, (and) caused it to be trod down by many elephants.

61

Bursting the earth, there arose a lotus-flower about th size of a wheel, shining with a pericarp of gems, effulgent with filaments of silver, having a row of petals of gold.

62

Standing on that lotus, which had a quantity of pollen spread about it by a gentle breeze, the relic of Buddha illumined the (different) quarters with its rays for a while.

63

People threw cloths and ornaments, caused a shower of flowers to rain, and filled the city with the noise of plaudits and expressions of approval.

64

The heretics, having afterwards made the king of kings believe that this was a great fraud, flung the relic on the surface of a ditch detestable owing to the dead bodies and the like (floating there).

65

At that moment the (ditch) became a pond like Nandá,[18] covered with the five kinds of lotus,[19] with multitudes of swans regaling there, and rendered delightful by the hum of rows of bees.

66

Elephants trumpeted; horses neighed; people uttered

plaudits; kettle-drums and the like struck a pleasant sound.

67

Men applauded it with songs of praise; even those who had modesty for (their) ornament[20] danced; those who were excited waved garments over their heads; those who had minds elated with joy clapped their hands.

68

The sky seemed as if it were overspread with clouds owing to the incense of the aloe-wood; the city appeared then as if made of cloth from the many lines of flags raised (over it).

69

Multitudes of ministers, gratified at seeing this incomprehensible miracle, went near King Pa*n*d*u*, and appealed to him in order to direct his attention to that which would tend to his benefit:—

70

"If any one witnessing such miraculous power of the supreme Sage, O king! experiences not even slight pleasure, of what advantage is his wisdom?

71

"The being pleased with qualities worthy of satisfaction is, O king! the characteristic of a virtuous man: when the moon rises, whole forests of water-lilies blossom[21] of their own accord.

72

"Owing to the word of those ignorant heretics, abandon not, O king! the path to heaven. What sensible man in search of a good road would travel taking blind men for his guides?

73

"Even the famous kings Kappina, Bimbisára, Suddhodana,[22] and the like, went to the King of the Law for refuge, and drank with reverence the nectar of his doctrines.

74

" Even the chief of the gods, the thousand-eyed,[23] finding his life drawing to a close, approached the eminent Sage who had overcome repeated births, heard his pure law, and attaining the bliss of the path (leading to Nibbána), received an extension of life.

75

" Thou also, O king of men! for the attainment of heaven and Nibbána, make speedily thy mind attached to the excellent King of the Law, the God of gods, who had overcome the five Máras."

76

The king, having listened to their speech, his doubts about the three gems dispelled, being of a joyful state of mind, addressed in the midst of his retinue the commander of the army who studied his welfare :—

77

" Not having faith in the virtue of the three gems which are the means of destroying repeated births, (and) walking in the path of heresy, for a long time I have been deceived, though (endowed) with supreme royal power.

78

" Suffering from cold, I have through ignorance blown a firefly whilst there was a fire burning; being thirsty, abandoning the water of the river, I have through heedlessness drunk the water of the mirage.

79

" Anxious to live long, I have, throwing away nectar, eaten malignant poison; casting away the garland of champac flower,[24] I have worn on my shoulders a necklace of snakes.

80

" Go quickly to the ditch, (and) having propitiated the tooth-relic of Buddha, bring it (hither); by rendering service (to it), I shall acquire the merit which produces happiness everywhere."

81

Then the commander of the army, greatly delighted, went to the ditch, and worshipping the relic of the Chief of sages, did what was serviceable to the king, and prayed as follows :—

82

"Having cast away the long-continued filth of heresy, the king has acquired faith in Sugata (Buddha); come thou to the palace of the king, (and) increase his good-will to the three gems."

83

At that time there sprang into existence a pond, charming with full-blown and golden lotuses, and adorning the sky like (the river) Mandákiní[25] that had newly descended (from heaven).

84

Then the relic of the eminent Sage, moving like a swan from lotus to lotus, made the entire city resemble the centre of the milky sea with rays white as the kunda flower.

85

Then the (relic), resting on the bright red lotus-like palm of the commander of the army, seen by great masses of the people, conferred great benefits on mankind.

86

The king, hearing this news, went on foot, with a joyful state of mind, making manifest twice as much pleasure as before, (and) astonished, spoke with clasped hands :—

87

"O supreme Sage! people skilled in trade set a price on valuable gold, having rubbed it on the touchstone; such is the custom observed from ancient times.

88

"Also, wise men having purified, by means of fire, a gem found in a good mine, place it as an ornament on the summit of a royal diadem.

89

"O supreme Sage! all this was done by me now for the purpose of testing thee. O thou of great wisdom! forgive my great sin, and quickly adorn my head."

90

Then the tooth-relic, resting on his diadem resplendent with the lustre of gems, emitted white rays, like streams of milk emanating from affection towards (the mother's offspring.)

91

The king, conveying the tooth-relic on his head, went round the city, his right side turned towards it,[26] (and), worshipping it with flowers and other necessaries, brought it to his well-decorated inner palace.

92

Placing the relic of Buddha on a most splendid throne, having a large white umbrella raised over it, and lustrous with gems, the king made an offering of gems and other precious stones.

93

The king, having to the end of his life found refuge in the three treasures, as Buddha and the rest, ceased injuring others, (and becoming) the abode of mercy, conciliated all people by his virtues.

94

The king caused also to be built for the relic a shrine shining with the splendour of various gems, as if it were the sun himself, suited to the weight of his piety, and decorated it in various ways.

95

He brought the relic to the relic temple; (and) adorning

the whole city, not satisfied with other acts of worship, he made an offering of his country, together with his wealth and possessions (to it).

96

Summoning before him King Guhasíva, and causing him to be honoured like himself, the eminent king, whose wealth consisted in piety, amassed many kinds of merit, such as the giving alms and the like.

97

Then the king, having given up the association with heretics—a source of evil—walking in the path easy to go by, owing to the light (shed on it) by the word of Buddha, skilled in (securing) his own and others' good, rendered eminent services to the world, having his people well-affected towards him by reason of his virtuous deeds.

CHAPTER IV.

1

Whilst this ruler of the earth was conducting himself in conformity with the duties of a sovereign, King Khíradhára, having an army inured to war, subduing the pride of his enemies by the display of his strong forces, inflated with pride resulting from the possession of immense resources, went forth ready for war.

2

Then the monarch—like as the king of lions, which has a mind free from fear, though it saw a mighty elephant[1] enter the passage to its cave—overwhelming with the great flood of an innumerable army the (other) king approaching the city, went to meet (him).

3

Pa*nd*u conquered Khíradhára in a great war, where the sky was obstructed with layers of thick dust which then arose, terror was caused by the preparation and noise of troops of various orders who were elated with pride, and torrents of rain of hundreds of sharp arrows abounded.

4

Then the eminent king, having secured the good-will of the people of his country, placed the burden of the kingdom on his own noble son, and intrusting the tooth-relic of Buddha to Guhasíva treated him well, (and) sent him to his own country.

5

The king, attaining the state of self-control for a long time, satisfied the poor with gifts of different kinds of wealth, (and), after the dissolution of his body, went to the assembly in the city of the gods, and received the great reward of merit he had desired.

6

King Guhasíva, bringing to his city the relic of the Chief of sages, honouring it much, and employing living beings in the path leading to happiness, passed his days storing up worthy and good deeds.

7

Prince Danta by name, the son of the king of Ujjení,[2] of immeasurable greatness, having commenced the observance of piety from a very early age, went to the great city of that king to worship the relic of the body of Him possessed of the ten powers.[3]

8

That prince, the abode of all goodness, made the king of Kalinga pleased with his virtues, performed duly acts of worship of different kinds, (and) lived there, daily reverencing the relic of Sugata.

9

There was a daughter of King Guhasíva, called Hemamálá,[4] having eyes like the full-blown water-lily, endowed with the gait of the swan, possessed of a countenance surpassing the lotus, bearing a large quantity of braided (and) lovely hair, and having a frame borne down by the weight of her breasts.

10

King Guhasíva, finding that the prince, the abode of all virtues, was fit to be (his) relation, (and) born of a very pure family, gave his daughter in great honour to that son of a king.

11

The king, having employed the prince, who had a large retinue, in the duty of protecting the relic in all ways, satisfied him with thousands of oxen, buffaloes, and the like, (and) established him in supreme power suited to his wealth.

12

King Khíradhára being killed in the field of battle, the princes who were his sister's sons, having repaired to the forest of Malaya,[5] and collected a powerful and great army, went near the city to seize the relic.

13

Then having pitched their camp near the city, they sent this message disagreeable to the ear—"Either give us the tooth-relic of Sugata, or instantly play the war-play which confers renown and prosperity."

14

Immediately, on hearing this message, the king said a word in secret to the prince—"Whilst my body lasts, I shall not give up the relic to another. Should I not be able to conquer them,

15

Take the tooth-relic adored by gods and men, (and) assuming the disguise of a Brahman, go to the island Síhala." Hearing thus the weighty instructions of his maternal uncle, the prince named Danta then addressed Guhasíva:—

16

"Who is there that is a relation of thine or mine in Síhala? or who is there that is pious towards the lotus-feet of Buddha? How could I take over the tooth-relic of Buddha to Síhala, which is but a small country on the other shore of the sea?"

17

(Then) Guhasíva spoke to the prince, the son of his sister, (thus):—"The relics of the body of Him possessed of the ten powers are already established in Síhala; the religion of the Teacher skilled in destroying the fear of (repeated) births flourishes (there); numberless priests also have lived (there).

18

"King Mahásena,[6] a dear friend of mine, devoted to the service of the two lotus-feet of Buddha, coveting even the water touched by a relic, sent me different kinds of gems as presents.

19

"That king, ever wise, is able to honour the tooth-relic of Sugata, worthy of honour, and to properly treat you, when separated from your accustomed country, with gifts of different kinds of wealth."

20

King Guhasíva, having thus persuaded the husband of his daughter, assembled his army, went to the battlefield, (and), fighting with the princes, fell under the power of death.

21

Then the prince named Danta, having heard the sad news respecting his maternal uncle, assumed the guise of a Brahman, and, taking the tooth-relic, fled in continued haste from the city.

22

And travelling quickly to the southern country,[7] being of a nature unmoved, he crossed a large and overflowing river by the influence of the gods, (and) buried the tooth-relic within a heap of sand.

23

Then returning to the city, and taking with him his wife, who had also assumed another disguise, he came (again) there quickly, and lived in a thicket, making offerings to the tooth-relic of Sugata buried in the heap of sand.

24

At that moment a Thera,[8] going in the skies, noticing a multitude of various rays rising thickly from the heap of sand where the relic was deposited, descended there, (and) worshipped the tooth-relic of Sugata.

25

Then the husband and wife, meeting there the son of the Sage,[9] being gratified, told him all the particulars of their journey. The son of Him possessed of the ten powers, bent on protecting the relic, (and) having a mind interested in the welfare of others, spoke to them both (as follows) :—

26

"Without minding the fatigue to the body, carry fearlessly this relic of the body of Him possessed of the ten powers to Síhala; and moreover, as soon as any difficulty arises in the way you go, think of me skilled in removing many dangers."

27

The wise son of Sugata, having thus spoken to the wife and husband, delivered also a religious discourse suited to them, (and) removing from them the dart of strong and deep grief, proceeded in the air to his abode.

28

Then a Nága king of the river, called Pa*nd*ubhára, of great power, living in the world of Nágas, leaving his own great city, (and) wandering whither he liked, arrived on that occasion at the place.

29

Observing a multitude of rays, lovely as the moon, rising from a heap of pure sand, he speculated (as to) what this (could be), and afterwards came to know that the relic of the Sage was in the heap of sand.

30

And being invisible, he swallowed instantly, (though) with much reverence, the casket made of gems which contained the relic, and, stretching out his body, entwined with the coils of his body the lofty (Meru),[10] king of golden-mountains, and laid himself down.

31

The husband and wife, desirous to go to sea, not finding the tooth-relic which had entered the sandy place, shed showers of tears caused by grief, (and) remembered at that moment the eminent son of Sugata.

32

Then the son of Sugata, knowing what was thought (by them), went near them who had their faces cast down by grief, and learnt that the relic of Buddha, though buried in the middle of a heap of sand and worshipped by the husband and wife, was not found (there).

33

Thereupon the eminent Thera saw by the power of his divine eyes the king of Nágas lying in an arbour at the mountain of gems.[11] In an instant he created for himself the body of a Garu*l*a, which covered the sky with large and spread-out wings.

34

Having, by the force of a powerful wind raised by his wings, divided in two the very deep sea, he ran quickly, causing terror, and reached the serpent-king lying at the foot of Meru.

35

Immediately the Nága chief, abandoning his snake-form, and, with a mind disturbed by fear, gathering up his hood, rushed forward quickly, made obeisance at his feet, and addressed the chief of the Theras a word sweet from its modesty :—

36

"Buddhas are born only for the benefit of all men ; even the worshipping of a relic is for the sake of good to mankind. I carried it away (thinking) thus—'I also, worshipping the relic of great price of Buddha, shall collect no small fruits of merit.'"

37

Then the king of Nágas, being told, "The relic is being taken to Síhala, the residence of multitudes of men who are able to comprehend the truth ; give up therefore the relic of the body of the eminent Sage," delivered the casket containing the relic.

38

The Thera, abandoning the body of the king of birds, rose from the ocean rendered frightful by hundreds of aquatic animals, (and) delivered to the husband and wife, who were descendants of kings, the relic, (even) as if it were the right of ruling the entire circle of the earth.[12]

39

The eminent Thera, who had thus conferred much favour, having departed, they, carrying the tooth-relic of Sugata on their heads, went thence, great and various acts of worship being performed on the road by the sylvan deities and other gods.

40

The road throughout had a gentle sweet-scented breeze, (and) free from thorns and the like; it was (also made) pleasant by its pure sand. The inhabitants of towns and cities paid due honours to them when they came to the road, by the influence of the tooth-relic.

41

Having travelled by a path rendered difficult by hills and forests, and always followed eagerly by the gods of the woods, who had their hands filled with flowers and scented powder, they slowly arrived at the city Támalitti.[13]

42

They suddenly saw a ship, made of planks fastened together, having a large (and) well-placed mast, a broad rising sail, and a skilful pilot, having merchants on board, going to the Lanká wished for by them.

43

Then the eminent Brahmans, going quickly near it, told the captain of the ship of their desire to go to Síhala. He, pleased in mind by their speech, which was agreeable to the ear, as also by their good demeanour, made them ascend the ship.

44

When they went to sea, taking with them the relic, the rows of rolling waves were becalmed; an even, scented, and pleasant north-wind blew; the (different) quarters also shone with a splendour spotless and lovely in every respect.

45

The ship, sailing uninterruptedly by the force of powerful

winds, like Garuta in the cerulean sky, entered the mid-ocean, which abounded in flowers of foam, and whence shore, mountains, and the like, ceased to be visible to the eyes.

46

The sea seemed to have a series of waves of the form of mountain-peaks, convulsed by frightful winds, (as) at the end of the world, (and) the sky to be disturbed by frightful sounds bursting the ears, and by the cries all night of men smitten with fear.

47

When at the end of the night the orb of the early sun rose on the summit of the eastern mountain, the water of the sea, with its rows of waves, was becalmed, (and) shone as if it were a cloth bedecked with emeralds.

48

To worship the relic of the body of the eminent Sage there rose Nágas,* some causing terror by the number of their outspread hoods; some endowed with divine forms, (and) holding in their hands sweet-smelling flowers; others carrying lovely gem-lamps; others bearing on their heads kanduppala (flowers;)[14]

49

Some wearing on their necks multitudes of full-blown water-lilies, some holding a number of golden vases, some bearing flags waving to the wind, some carrying in their hands caskets filled with lovely gold powder;

50

Some performing a dance with gestures graceful (and) pleasing to the mind; some singing songs, sweet and in equal cadence with the dance; some playing on various musical instruments.

51

The tooth-relic of the eminent Sage, ascending to the sky from the massy and lovely hair of the princess, as if it were

* *Vide* end, 50th verse.

the digit of the moon emerging from the interior of a blue cloud, emitted rays resembling straight darts of silver.

52

The sky seemed as if it had not sufficient space for the sounds of approval[15] and the like, which, pregnant with echoes, were uttered by the Nágas, who, with minds pleased, witnessed on that occasion the unequalled power of the relic.

53

The tooth-relic of Sugata afterwards descended from the sky, (and) entered the massed hair[16] of the princess; multitudes of Nágas stopped the ship, (and) made great offerings for seven nights and days.

54

The husband and wife, finding the ship motionless in the middle of the sea, like an immovable divine mansion in the sky, their minds agitated by fear, consulting together, remembered the powerful son of Him possessed of the ten powers.

55

The son of the Sage, instantly knowing their thought, appeared, treading a cluster of clouds in the sky, and assuming the great body of the king of birds, speedily drove away the Nágas smitten with fear.

56

When the son of Buddha departed, having thus removed the fear caused by the Nágas, the ship, with flags stirred by the wind, dividing the high wave-lines, which were large and resembled a series of clouds, bore down quickly, by the influence of the Thera, (and) with the speed of motion, to the city of Lanká.[17]

CHAPTER V.

1

Then, in the ninth year of (the reign of) King Kittisirimegha, the son of Mahásena, they, the husband and wife,[1] having arrived at that city, lived in a delightful temple.

2

An eminent Brahman, having met those travellers at night, satisfied them with delicious food and drink, and then at the end of the night pointed out to the husband and wife the road to Anurádhapura.[2]

3

Afterwards, being (thus) respectfully treated by the worthy Brahman, they took the eminent tooth-relic of Buddha, left the city, and, completing their journey over a very long road, reached the suburbs of Anurádhapura.

4

If, in the expectation of seeing any pious king the husband and wife came to that country, they heard (instead) that Mahásena, king of Lanká, had died long ago of a disease which attacked him.

5

Overwhelmed by grief, as by a mountain which had suddenly sprung up, being foolish, they lamented much (his death); all directions and intermediate points[3] appeared then to them, fainting in their minds, to be heavy with darkness.

6

The husband and wife, hearing of the devotion to the three gems of King Kittisirimegha, who was then established in rule, were released from the heat of grief, as a forest in heavy fire is quenched by rain.

7

Being told of the friendship (with the king) of a certain priest (living) at the great monastery called Meghagiri,[4] they both unanimously went to him, accepted the hospitality done to them, and told him of the news of the relic.

8

That eminent sage, learning the news of the tooth-relic, was pleased, as if his body had been sprinkled over with nectar, and lodged at once the stainless relic in his house adorned with canopies of cloth.

9

And he, having greatly honoured them both, husband and wife sent, according to their wish, a priest to the king of Lanká, to communicate to him those pleasant tidings.

10

The king, enjoying sport on a certain day in spring-time, with his queens in the royal park, saw at a distance the priest coming there with a bright colour on his face.

11

The priest, having approached the king, communicated to him the news, with a pleased mind. Having heard it, he bore the burden of immense happiness, like one who had obtained the Chakka gem.[5]

12

The King of Lanká knew that the saying of the expounder of omens[6] was true when he spoke thus :—" Two Brahmans, husband and wife, carrying the tooth-relic of Buddha, will, with one mind, come to Lanká before long."

13

Immediately, then, the pious and glad-hearted king went on foot, with a large retinue, to the monastery Meghagiri, in the north-east direction of Anurádhapura.

14

Beholding the relic of Sugata difficult to be obtained, wetting his necklace of beautiful pearls with an abundance of tears caused by joy, he made obeisance (to it) in great veneration, and thought thus, the down of his body bristling up (with joy) :—

15

"Though I should offer to-day my head, difficult to give away and bearing a diadem resplendent with many gems, to Buddha, the sole refuge of the world, I should not be making an offering befitting the relic.

16

"No man of sane mind in this world would think—'I am making an offering suitable to Him, offering even the whole circle of the earth, with its many treasures, wealth, and enjoyments.'

17

"This dominion of mine in Lanká is but very small; but Buddha is illimitable in virtues of various kinds. How can I, of little wealth, honour such a being, who is possessed of the ten powers, the sole Chief of the three worlds?"

18

Thus, again and again thinking of the same matter, he, though endowed with courage, fainted away. Being quickly fanned by his distressed servants with the air from the Chámara,[7] he regained consciousness.

19

"Wise men, planting even a small seed in the great earth, enjoy in due time many wished for results, such as leaves, bark, flowers, fruits, and the like.

20

"In this manner, making even a very small offering to the Lord of the Law, who is illimitable in virtues of various kinds,

I shall obtain the incomparable happiness of heaven and Nibbána, delightful owing to the ripening of merit in the course of time."[8]

21

Having thought thus, the king, endowed with a face like the full moon, offered, through excessive weight of joy, all this island of Síhala to the excellent tooth-relic of the Omniscient.

22

Then priests, wise and skilled in the Tipiṭaka,[9] Játaka, Logic, Agáma, and the like, and citizens who had their sole refuge in the three treasures, assembled there instantly through curiosity.

23

The king, in the midst of a great retinue, spoke thus—"The eminent Sage was possessed of very white teeth. If the teeth of Buddha were white like the planet Venus, why is this stained with dirt?"

24

At that moment the tooth-relic of the King of sages, with two wings outspread like a royal swan, and having numerous rays dispersed in the sky, rushed quickly, whirling about for a moment's time.

25

The king, having spread a very costly white carpet, placed the relic of the Sage on a splendid seat, and covered it with clusters of jessamine flowers, of a colour like that of the clouds at the close of the rainy season.

26

Then the relic of the Chief of sages, having quickly risen, stood on the top of the heap of flowers, and shone with milk-white rays, causing the eyes of beholders to cease to twinkle.

27

From a desire to test it again, he placed the relic on a silk cloth—resembling the line of foam in the milky sea—

spread over the seat, (and) covered it with many hundreds of cloths of great value.

28

The relic, rising immediately, burst through the hundreds of cloths, like the moon emerging from the interior of a white cloud, and, planting itself on them, made all the (different) quarters irradiant with rays white as the kunda flower.

29

At that moment the earth, together with its mountains, roared, as if to give utterance to an expression of approval. Also, as if to witness the wonder, the sea became becalmed, the arms of its waves (reposing) in tranquillity.

30

Divine flowers fell from the sky, as from a tree in full blossom shaken by a furious elephant; in the sky, goddesses exhibited to the people their wonderful skill in dancing.

31

Divine singers sang songs, pleasing from the high tunes arising from their merriment; divine musical instruments played upon emitted a twofold, high, and sweet melody.

32

The earth and sky were knitted together by a cloud with hundreds of raindrops, resembling hundreds of silver cords; all directions were thoroughly irradiated with lightning-lamps in the midst of great festoons of clouds.

33

There blew also gently a cold wind, which had shaken the forest in the Malaya mountains, lovely from its bearing aloft the pollen of full-blown flowers, (and) capable of removing large quantities of perspiration-drops.

34

The king, having witnessed this rare miracle, (and) the

great festival of the people, such as was never seen before, kept his two eyes unshut, by reason of intense happiness, (and) made a large offering of gems and other objects.

35

Then, carrying the relic on his head, he stood on a splendid chariot, which had a white umbrella raised over it, a variegated coverlet (spread on it), and white horses yoked to it, and entered Anurádhapura, the abode of prosperity.

36

The king, possessed of unequalled powers, deposited the relic of the Sage on a throne having a white umbrella held above it, (and) a white woollen coverlet spread on it, in his house, well adorned (even) like the palace of Indra.

37

The king, longing for happiness and heaven,[10] constructed a relic-temple of great value in (his palace, and) placing there the relic of the supreme Sage, honoured it day and night with many kinds of gifts.

38

The chief of the threefold Síhala, being pleased, treated them both, husband and wife, kindly, (and) presented to them many gems, ornaments and villages where distinguished families only can reside.

39

The inhabitants of provinces, market-towns, cities, and the like, having assembled, felt aggrieved at not seeing the relic of Sugata, (and) praising highly the deeds of the Chief of the world, made a loud clamour in the presence of the king, saying :—

40

" The Lord of the Law was born in the world for the benefit of all people; he did good to all mankind; his relics were presented for the benefit of the mass; we are anxious to make offerings to the relic."

41

The king, summoning the council of priests living in the grove near Anurádhapura, made known the wish of the assembled people to worship the relic of Buddha.

42

In that great congregation of priests, a Thera, unequalled in the power of his understanding, the abode of kindness, said thus to the king of the threefold Síhala, who was of great wisdom, skilled in doing good to the world :—

43

"The securing the advantage of people dependent on one is certainly a virtue put into constant practice by great men. Bring out the relic in the spring season, (and) show it to the people, who wish (to perform) acts of merit."

44

Having heard the well-spoken words of the eminent sage, the king asked the assembled priests again :—"For this vast mass of people to worship the relic, what very pleasing place is here?"

45

Then all the priests living in the monasteries,[11] through attachment, each spoke highly of his own place. Their words differing from each other, the king was neither much pleased with any (of their) words, nor did he reject them.

46

But the king, having come to an impartial state in his own mind, spoke again in the midst of the assembly of priests (thus) :—"The relic of the Chief of sages will go instantly of its own accord to a place adapted for it."

47

Then the king, going to his palace, quickly opened the multitude of lotus-faces[12] of the people who were desirous of worshipping the relic, and ordered the city and the road to the monastery to be decorated.

48

The street was well swept, the dust kept down by the sprinkling of water; it was (made) very pleasant by the strewing of sand (over it); (and) triumphal arches, beautified with gold and set with images of tigers and the like, were erected.

49

A row of flags warded off the heat of the sun by their shade, (and) appeared, as if dancing; the street from its colour, assumed the appearance of a forest-line of rows of full-grown plantain-trees[13] in spring-time.

50

New vases filled (with water)[14] indicated to good men that the wished-for happiness of heaven and Nibbána will be attained. Moreover, the clear day became cloudy owing to the incense emanating from camphor, frankincense, and aloe-wood.

51

Temporary pavilions of various kinds, (adorned) with pendant necklaces of white pearls, were erected there, and festoons of flowers, with crowds of bees fond of fragrance buzzing about them, were (also) made.

52

Some went to the festival wearing beautiful robes; some bearing in their hands baskets filled with flowers; other people carrying loads of fragrant powder; others (again) holding large umbrellas beautified in various ways.

53

Then the lord of Lanká, placing the relic of the Chief[15] of the three worlds in a splendid chariot yoked to horses white as the moon and shining with the brilliance of gems, having first made obeisance (to it), said this word :—

54

"O Chief of sages! (as thou didst go) to the terrace of the Bodhi-tree to attain Buddhahood, to the tree Ga*nd*amba to subdue the heretics, to Migadáya[16] to expound the Law, go also to-day, of thine own accord, to a place where it will be fit to honour thee."

55

Then the king, skilled in performing acts suited to the occasion, let the royal chariot proceed without a charioteer in it; he himself went afterwards, with a great retinue, making offerings unequalled in their kind.

56

The city looked like the sea raging (at the end of the world), owing to the shouts of applause from a large concourse of people, the outspread neighings of horses, the beating of drums, and the loud trumpeting of elephants.

57

Ladies of rank ran in exultation to the two sides of the streets, threw golden ornaments, caused a shower of flowers to rain on all sides, (and) waved garments over their heads.

58

On the chariot coming near the eastern gate, like a ship going over the surface of the sea, multitudes of priests and all men, being pleased, worshipped it there with various gifts.

59

Then the splendid chariot having gone round the city with its right side turned towards it, came out at the northern gate, (and) stood, like a ship with goods arrived at a harbour, in a place which had been made pure by the religious discourse of the sage Mahinda.[17]

60

The king of Lanká, taking out at that place the eminent tooth-relic of Buddha from within the casket decorated with gems, like the moon from an evening cloud, exhibited it to the inhabitants of provinces, towns, (and) cities.

61

The people, filled instantly with very great joy, caused a shower of ornaments and objects of value to rain on it, and the mouths of the (different) quarters were made to resound with festive songs composed by rejoicing bards.

62

Numerous lotus-like hands of the people were clasped together as at the rising of the moon; countless expressions of approval uttered in the sky by Brahmas, gods, and the like, spread even through the centre of the world.

63

The tooth-relic, of a colour like a part of the moon, white as the kunda flower and new sandal-wood, caused with its radiance palace gates, mountains, trees, and the like, to appear for a moment as if they were formed of polished silver.

64

Who, witnessing this incomprehensible and great miracle in that place, did not feel his hair standing on end? Or who carried home each his ornaments? or who did not (then) enjoy the privilege of existence?

65

Who did not (then) renounce the long persistent defilement of heresy? Or who did not wish to witness the greatness of Buddha? or who were indeed then bound in the meshes of avarice? or who did not then seek the three treasures for protection?

66

The king of Lanká also having worshipped the incomparable relic of the Omniscient, enlarged again the abode of the tooth-relic at an expenditure of ninety thousand (pieces of gold, and) honoured it daily in the inner palace.

67

Carrying the relic every year to the monastery Abhayuttara,[18] that king called Kittisirimegha, observant of truth, caused a record to be written of what he had done, for the purpose of securing offerings of that nature to it.

68

The chiefs of the earth, with Buddhadása[19] at their head, and others also,—observing this custom, pleasing from their being endowed with excellent qualities, such as piety and kindness, as their ornaments,—honoured the tooth-relic of Buddha in many ways.

69

Recognising the advantage secured to men by the Teacher in many past births (of his), believing in his Buddhahood, which removes all sinful passions, giving ear to his excellent Law, and seeking the association with good men, a man of keen intellect should be anxious to attain the tranquil Nibbána, the means of dissipating the fear of the three births.

HISTORY OF THE AUTHOR.

6[1]

This history of the tooth-relic of Buddha, which gives delight to the hearers, (and) is a lamp for (displaying) the power of the All-seeing, was composed by the royal teacher called Dhammakitti, whose wealth was piety, and who was soft-worded;

1

Who wrote a splendid *Tíká*[2] for the Panchiká on the excellent grammar made by Chandagomi, and a *Tíká* for the commentary on the Vinaya (called) Samantapásádiká, which imparts strength to the understanding;

2

Who composed a *Tíká* for the commentary on the noble scripture Anguttara,[3] which destroys ignorance and misapprehension; and also a work called Vinayasangaha for the benefit of numerous priests, zealous in the observance of the sacred ordinances;

5

Who was of a pure race, possessed of much kindness and other virtuous qualities, skilled in logic and the sacred sciences, bold, with a wide renown like unto a multitude of moonbeams spread everywhere, and considerate;

4

(Also) a pupil of the great and venerable Sáriputta,[4] born of a pure race, occupying the highest office of a teacher of all sciences, versed in all the various systems of religions;[5]

3

Of subdued organs, devoted to the sacred laws, fond of a

life of subjugated passions, of tranquil mind, wearing as his ornaments combined virtues, (such as) contentment and the like, and the means of (furthering) the progress of the religion of Buddha.

7

May the religion of the supreme Sage last long! May kings be established in justice! May rain fall in (due) season! May all people attain happiness by exercising mutual friendliness!

NOTES.

CHAPTER I.

1. *The Teacher* (*vide* also Note 23).—One of the numerous designations of Buddha. He is the Teacher of *Paramattha*, or preeminent truth as propounded in his *Dhamma* or Law.

2. *The Three Worlds*.—These are (1.) The World of Senses; (2.) The World of Form; (3.) The World of No-Form; and are unlike the Hindu Three Worlds—viz., the Middle, the Higher, and the Lower Worlds.

3. *Dhamma* is here rendered as "*the Law.*" I have sometimes translated it also as "the Doctrine."

4. *Vijjá*.—These are made up of the following eight attributes, viz.:—(1.) Abstract meditation; (2.) The power to assume any form at will; (3.) Magical power; (4.) Supernatural power of hearing; (5.) The capability to know what is in the mind of others; (6.) Supernatural power of seeing; (7.) The extinction of desires (*Kilesa*); (8.) The knowledge of what took place in previous states of existence.

5. *Charana*.—These consist of fifteen attributes, viz.:—(1.) Moral life; (2.) Subjugation of the passions; (3.) Temperance in meals; (4.) Vigilance; (5.) Faith; (6.) Shame; (7.) Fear of sin; (8.) Study; (9.) Courage; (10.) Memory; (11.) Wisdom; (12, 13, 14, 15.) Four kinds of *Jhánas* or abstract meditation.

6. *Papancha*.—Equivalen to Sanskrit *Prapancha*—delusion, deceit. It also means the developed world with its delusions and vanities.

7. *Saññojana*.—These are the ten bonds, such as different kinds of desire or heresy, which bind a man to repeated births. They are divided into two sets of five each, called "*Orambhagiya*" and "*Uddhambhágiya*." 1. *Orambhagiya*, those which relate to this world, viz.:—(1.) *Sakkáyaditthi*; (2.) *Vichikichchhá*; (3.) *Sílabbataparámasa*; (4.) *Kámarága*; (5.) *Vyápáda*. 2. *Uddhambhágiya*, those which relate to the other world, viz.:—

(1.) *Rúparága;* (2.) *Aruparága;* (3.) *Mána;* (4.) *Uddhachcha;* (5.) *Avijjá.* Those who are endowed with the first five are born in the world of senses; those endowed with the next five, in the higher worlds; and those who are encumbered with neither of the two sets attain Nibbána. Refer to *Vibhanga* and *Súchilôma.*

8. *Sangha.*—Prof. Max Müller (in the *Dhamma Pada*), translates this word as "Church." Its strict meaning is association, assembly, council. Buddhistic works generally invoke Buddha, his Law, and his Church or *Sangha,* in their prefatory verses. They are also called "the three Gems" or "the three Treasures."

9. *Achchuta.*—This word means immovable, deathless, and designates here the state of Nibbána.

10. *Kálaka Nágara.*—The pedigree of this (*Kshatriya*) warrior family is given in the *Maháwansa.*

11. 5 *and* 6.—In Oriental languages several verses sometimes run into each other in such a manner that it is difficult to separate them in a translation. Hence here, as elsewhere, two or three verses are rendered together.

12. *Lanká.*—The classic name for Ceylon. It means "the resplendent."

13. *Lílávatí* was the wife of *Parakkama Báhu I.*, a renowned king of Ceylon. She reigned as queen at *Pollanaruva* three times, and was dethroned as many times. According to Turnour, she ruled in the following years:—

First, . .	1197–1200 A.D.
Secondly, .	1209–1210 "
Thirdly, . .	1211–1211 "

This work is supposed to have been composed during the last reign of *Lílávatí.*

14. *Pandu.*—In Southern India there reigned three lines of Tamil kings, the *Chola, Chera,* and *Pándian* dynasties, respectively at Tanjore, Travancore, and Madura. The *Pándians* were more or less connected with Ceylon, and the Tamils of the *Pándian* kingdom colonised extensively the north and east of the island. Latterly the kings of Kandy came from Madura, whilst many a Tamil or Telegu princess also left her home in India to become the queen-consorts of the Ceylon kings. From Tamil writings we learn that one or two of the *Pándian* kings of Madura were also Buddhists. The struggles for supremacy between Brahmanism and Buddhism in the Tamil-land of India are described in some parts of the *Tiruvatavúr Purána.* In olden times the communication between Ceylon and India was maintained chiefly through the Sinhalese kingdoms of *Anuradhapura* and *Pollanaruva* on the one hand, and that of Madura on the

other. From the phraseology occasionally adopted in this Pali work by the author, it is easy to infer that the influence of the Tamil connection was to some extent felt also by the Sinhalese literature of that epoch.

15. *Giving whatever was asked of her.*—According to Oriental ideas, profuse liberality is one of the great characteristics of a king. In this respect King *Karna* of the *Mahá Bhárata* is the Indian model. When asked by Krishna, at the point of death in the battlefield, to make also a gift of the reward due to all his meritorious deeds, Karna readily complied with even this request, and only then gave up his ghost, ready to face the new world denuded of "the riches he had stored up in the heavenly mansions."

16. *Parakkama Báhu.*—(*Vide* Note 13.)

17. *Kalá, Arts.*—These were sixty-four, such as archery, horsemanship, the riding of elephants, the driving of chariots, acting, dancing, music, grammar, prosody, astronomy, &c., in which Indian princes were expected to be proficient.

18. *Threefold Síhala.*—Síhala means Ceylon, the land of the Sinhalese. It was in ancient times divided into three parts, called *Rôhana*, *Máya*, and *Patitthá.*

19. *And the like.*—This is the rendering of *Ádi*, a word which occurs repeatedly in this book. It is equivalent in some degree to the European *etcetera*, and yet it means something more. When a word ends with *Ádi*, the author means a great deal more, which he wishes to be understood. It literally means, "and other things, *beginning with* the word mentioned." It is so commonly used amongst Orientals, that the repetition of it in their conversation or writing does not jar on the ears as its frequent use is likely to do in an English translation. I have attempted to diversify the translation by rendering it in different ways, such as, "and other things," "and other requisites," &c., being chiefly guided by the context.

20. *Like the moon.*—The moon furnishes a great storehouse for metaphor to Indian poets. He (for the moon is of the masculine gender in Indian languages) is the paragon of beauty and gentleness, and renowned for such.

21. *Mágadhí language.*—Another name for *Pali*, derived from the country of *Mágadha* (Behar), in which it was chiefly spoken.

22. *Other islands also.*—According to Buddhistic and Indian cosmogony, the world was composed of several islands. Even India, or *Jambudípa*, as it is called, was considered to be only an island.

23. *The Conqueror.*—*Jina* means this. To avoid tautology, the Pali poet calls Buddha by a variety of names, such as *Jina*,

Sugata, *Tathágata*, *Satthá*, *Muni*, the lord of the three worlds, &c., each descriptive of some special attribute of his. To prevent a confusion of ideas, the reader of the translation should bear this in mind.

24. *Vedángas.*—This means the "limbs" of the Vedas. In Southern India these have been rendered to mean those sciences and books required to be studied for the proper understanding of the Vedas, such as grammar, prosody, &c. But others would make the *Upanishads*, &c., fall also under this term. The Buddhistic scriptures, however, had nine *angas*, or divisions of their own.

25. *Amara.*—This is supposed to be the same as *Amarávatí.* But there is also an *Amarápuri* known to the Hindus as the mythical city of *Alekésa*, the god of wealth.

26. *Repeated births.*—*Bhava* means this. The aim of all Indian philosophy and religion is to overcome the necessity for existence in a succession of births or a state of transmigration.

27. *Left his home.*—Abandoning the householder's life and becoming an ascetic, was an everyday custom of ancient Hindu life, and is not quite unknown even in the present day. In fact, it was considered the right way of concluding one's earthly career, and formed the two last stages of a Hindu's life, called *Vánapprastha* and *Sanyása.*

28. *Himáchala* means the same as the Himalaya, the "snowy" mountain.

29. *King of gods.*—This is *Indra*, who is also called *Sakka.*

30. *In transcendent knowledge*, *i.e.*, in the five *Abhinnás*, which are somewhat like the *Vijjá* already described.

31. *Meditation.*—This is the rendering adopted for *Samádhi*, which is a state of abstraction of the mind, where all one's thoughts being stilled, the Ego rests in contemplation of itself, as part of the great unknown, and thereby loses ultimately its egoism itself. This was the central idea of the Indian *Samádhi;* but the Buddhistic *Samádhi* differed from it in some material respects. Yet both kinds of *Samádhi* agreed in this essential—viz., the arresting of all thought and the suppression of the breath as a means of effecting this object. There are several stages to be attained in a *Samádhi*, which, in truth, was considered as a foretaste in this world of the heaven or *Nibbána* to be attained in the other. *Jhana* also meant religious meditation of this nature.

32. *Dípankara Buddha.*—One of the twenty-four Buddhas who preceded *Gotama Buddha* or the last Buddha, to which this work refers. To enlighten the world, every now and then a Buddha appears. The one next expected is called *Metteyya Buddha.* The world is believed at present to be under the dispensation of *Gotama Buddha.*

33. *Rahats* is rendered as saints. They are the sanctified sages of Buddhism, who have reached the stage of *Arahattam*, having passed through the other three stages of *Sotápatti*, *Sakadágámi*, and *Anágámi*.

34. *Ramma.*—Possibly the same as *Rámagama* on the Ganges.

35. *Tathágata.*—Another name for Buddha. The word means, literally, "thus gone." Gotama is also a *Tathágata*, as, like the previous Buddhas, he will be gone for ever, and never return to be born again in this world of woe. (*Vide* Turnour's Introduction, pages 55 and 56.)

36. *Páramí virtues.*—These are the ten virtues, the attainment of which is indispensable for acquiring the status of a Buddha. And they are:—(1.) *Dana*, alms-giving; (2.) *Síla*, moral conduct; (3.) *Nikkamána*, secluded life; (4.) *Panna*, wisdom; (5.) *Viriya*, persevering courage; (6.) *Khanti*, patience; (7.) *Sachcha*, truthfulness; (8.) *Adhitthána*, resolution; (9.) *Metta*, kindness; (10.) *Upekkha*, equanimity or toleration.

37. *Asankheyyas.*—Literally, what is uncountable, innumerable. It is numeral 1, followed by one hundred and forty ciphers.

38. *Kappas.*—Vast periods or cycles of time. In Sanskrit, *Kalpa*. During these cycles the universe is subjected to alternate processes of destruction and renovation.

39. *Tusita.*—There are six heavens, and of these *Tusita* is the fourth, where *Bodhisattas*, or beings destined to become Buddhas, live.

40. *For his wealth compassion*, *i.e.*, the only riches he valued or possessed was kindness, love, mercy, &c.

41. *Surádhipas.*—This word in the plural means the eight chiefs of the *Suras*, or gods, such as, *Indra*, *Yama*, *Agni*, *Váyu*, *Varuna*, &c.

42. *Chakkaválas.*—A sphere of worlds. There are several such scattered in the universe, each having its own planetary system.

43. *Suddhodana.*—King of a part of Ayodhia (Oude), and a tributary of the king of *Kosala*.

44. *Matchless chief.*—The literal rendering of the Pali words would be "the only banner-chief," meaning a king who had a peerless banner. The Indian monarchs, and even their gods, had each a characteristic flag.

45. *Sakya race.*—These were descendants of *Iksváku*, and formed a branch of the solar dynasty, who reigned in the *Sakya* country.

46. *Kapila.*—Equal to *Kapila Vasthu*, the site of *Kapila*. *Iksváku* drove some of his sons away from his kingdom. They went near the *Himalaya* mountains, and built a city there, with the permission of the sage *Kapila*. Hence the name. It was in *Ayodhia*, and Buddha was born in it.

47. *Uttered a fearless expression.*—This indicates that by his voice he made it appear that he was not afraid of any tempter or temptation. In battle, the Indian warriors began the war always with such expressions, called *Sinha Nátha,* uttered on either side, which the Indian poets are careful to record.

48. *Siddhattha Kumára, i.e.,* the prince who has actually attained success in what he wished.

49. *Channaka.*—The name of the prime minister. His life is given in *Anguttara Atthakathá.* He was a very haughty man once, but when converted to Buddhism, he became gentle and good, and passed his days preaching at *Kósambi.*

50. *Anôma.*—A river in the *Sakya* country, and a branch of the Ganges.

51. *Chúlámani.*—Equal to *Chúdámani* in Sanskrit. It signifies literally a "crown-jewel." It means also a monument of the shape of an Indian crown, which is of different form from that of the European crown, and was somewhat conical. This was also the style of the Buddhistic topes.

52. *Yôjanas.*—A measure of distance, equal to sixteen English miles.

53. *Ghatíkára.*—Literally a "pot-maker." Here it is the name of a Brahma who it is said was originally a pot-maker. But it must be borne also in mind that some of the philosophic poets of India designate God and also Brahma as a "pot-maker," *i.e.,* one who creates the world out of the "clay of matter." The *Gatika Sutta,* in the *Majjhima Nikaya,* gives an account of the life and antecedents of this Brahma, who brought the *yellow robes,* which were ochre-coloured robes worn by Indian ascetics. The colour of the robe of the Buddhists was more yellowish. *Kasáya* is the name of the colour of the clothes adopted by the Hindus.

54. *Cloth monument* is the literal rendering of *Dussachetiya,* so called either from its being made of cloths or from Buddha's robe being preserved there.

55. *Mahápadhána* means great efforts, great perseverance. It is not very unlike the Vedantic *Vyrákkia.*

56. *The full moon.*—The full moon is a day of great sanctity amongst the Hindus. The Buddhists treat it with equal veneration. Even in their modern usages the Buddhists attach great importance to this day, their great religious festivals being fixed for the full moon. Also, Indian magicians consider their incantations doubly efficacious when performed on this day.

57. *Bodhi-tree.*—Each Buddha sits in meditation under the shade of a tree, and attains Buddhahood. Hence it is called the tree of Buddhahood, or *Bodhi*-tree. Gotama Buddha's *Bodhi*-tree was a *ficus religiosa.* A branch of it is yet believed to grow at

Anurdáhapura in Ceylon, having been planted there in 288 B.C. Every Buddhist temple now has a *ficus religiosa* growing within its confines. Childers writes that the *Bodhi*-tree occupies in modern Buddhism the same position as the cross in Christianity.—*Courageous.*—The Pali word is *Víriya*, a well-known word in Indian philosophy. According to the Buddhists, there are four kinds of *Víriya* or persevering courage, according as it is kept up till (1.) the skin, (2.) the nerves, (3.) the bones, and (4.) the blood and flesh are withered up.

58. *Mára* is not the Sanskrit *Káma*, but the appellation for gods or evil spirits of the sixth heaven. The word is also used to designate the evil principle, the tempter, the hindrances to the attainment of heaven. There are five *Máras* according to Buddhists, but here the word means only *Devaputtamára*, evil gods.

59. *Asuras.*—Opposed to *Suras*, the gods. Both *Suras* and *Asuras* came into existence at "the churning of the milky ocean." The former were the good gods, and the latter the evil gods. They are also called *Yavanas* in the *Skanda Purána*, which describes the origin of these two sets of beings, and the tremendous wars waged between them.

60. *The lowest and other hells.*—*Avíchi* is one of the eight hells, which were—(1.) *Sanjíva;* (2.) *Kála Sutta;* (3.) *Mahá Roruva;* (4.) *Roruva;* (5.) *Páthapara;* (6.) *Avíchi;* (7.) *Sangháta;* and (8.) *Tápana.* (Consult *Padípiká.*)

61. *Petas* were evil spirits, who, ever greedy of eating and drinking, and yet unable to gratify their appetites, were in a constant state of hunger and thirst.

62. *Bodily ornaments.*—The poet wishes to intimate that even insensible objects felt delighted, and gave outward signs of their joy.

63. *A double miracle*, or "a pair of miracles," would be the rendering of *Yamaka.* These miracles should be opposed to each other, such as fire and water, light and darkness, heat and cold.

64. *The seat of victory.*—The victory alluded to here is the subjugation of the *Máras*, or the tempters.

65. *Sámanta Patthána.*—This is the name of the seventh and last book of the *Abhidhamma* (the third part of the Buddhistic *Tipitaka*), which consists of discourses relating to transcendental and metaphysical subjects. It is the most important of all the seven books.

66. *Ajapála* means literally cowkeeper or goatkeeper. Possibly cows and sheep found shelter under this banyan-tree.

67. *Muchalinda* is the *Barringtonia acutangula.*

68. *Rájáyatana* is the Indian iron-wood tree, called also the *Pála*-tree.—"*The thousand-eyed God*" is Indra. (*Vide* Note 23, Chap. III.)

69. *Tapassu and Bhalluka.*—These were the two first to believe in Buddha.

70. *Sahampati.*—Another name for *Brahma*, one of the Hindu triad.

71. *Báránasí* is modern Benares.

72. *Isipatana.*—Literally "the place where the sages stood." It was in the vicinity of Benares. Buddha's first discourse was delivered there.—*The unvarying place.*—This means that all Buddhas, before and after *Gotama*, have to be seated on this particular spot in *Isipatana*, to preach their law and dispensation.

73. *Wheel of the Law.* — "*Dhamma Chakka*," Childers writes (Dictionary, p. 216), should be rendered by some such expression as "the reign of religion, the dominion of the Law." Turnour translates it as "the sovereign supremacy of the Law." It is a stock phrase of Buddhism, and indicates the propagation and triumph of that religion.

74. *Añña Kondañña.*—A Brahman who became the first Buddhist priest. When Buddha's father asked him as to the future of his son, he predicted that he would become a Buddha, and patiently awaited that event, and became a convert to his religion.

75. *The doctrine of the Paths, i.e.*, of the four leading to Nibbána, *Sotápanno, Sakádágami, Anágámi*, and *Arahá.*

CHAPTER II.

1. *Phussa* is equal to the last part of December and the beginning of January.

2. *Yakkhas.*—Those who inhabited Ceylon before it was settled by the Hindus from Northern India, who were led thither by Vijaya. The *Yakkhas* were also supposed to be a class of demons. Could there be any connection between this term and the *Rákshasas*, or giants, who, according to the *Rámayana*, inhabited Ceylon, and to conquer whose king (Rávana), Ráma made an expedition to the island? Turnour thinks that *Yakkha* is derived from the root *Yaja*, to make offerings.

3. *Mahánágavana.*—The present *Mahyangana*, in Bintenne, near Badulla, where Buddhistic temples and monuments are yet in existence.

4. *Giridípa.*—An island in which the *Yakkhas* were floated away from Ceylon.

5. *Kotis.*—A *koti* is equal to ten millions.

6. *Mahásumana.*—The same as the god *Sumana*, who has a temple at Ratanapura, and is worshipped by the Buddhists there. He is supposed to be *Lakshmana*, the brother of *Ráma*.

7. *Sumanakúta* is called now *Sripáda*, or Adam's Peak. Mr W. Skeen has written an interesting book about it. The footprint on the peak is worshipped by Hindus, Buddhists, and Mohammedans alike, each claiming it to be that of their own god. It is one of the highest mountains in the island. The priest attached to the temple on the peak is a man of great importance. The present incumbent, *Sumangala*, is a very learned Pali scholar.

8. *Jetavana.*—The name of a park in *Ayodhia* (Oude). It was purchased by *Anáthapindika* (*vide* Chap. III., v. 28, 29) from Prince *Jeta*, and dedicated to Buddha. Hence its name. Many of his discourses were delivered here.

9. *Thúpa.*—Equal to *Sthúpa* in Sanskrit. A tope, or dagóba, being a monument or mausoleum of a conical shape.

10. *Nágas.*—Literally, snakes. But the word means more than this—a species of human beings who had the hoods of snakes, with three, five, or seven heads. They had the power to assume any form they liked. The Nága princesses were reputed to be great beauties, and many a marriage between the kings of the East and these princesses, who lived in the world below, or *Pátala*, are recounted in the Indian legends and *Puránas*. The *Nágas* each possessed a gem of pre-eminent lustrousness and value set on the hoods. Very great intimacy appears to have existed between men and the *Nágas*. Their kings are alleged to have come in state from the infernal regions to assist at the festivals of Indian kings. They have even sometimes taken part in their wars. In short, the *Nágas*, whoever they were, have played an important part in Indian mythology and history. (Consult *Vidhura Jataka*.)

11. *Nágadípa.*—The island of the Nágas. Some islands near Jaffna, in the north of Ceylon, are yet called *Nagadivu*, where temples are dedicated to a *Nága Thampirán*, or snake-god. The images worshipped in them are those of snakes. *Nágadípa* is, however, supposed to be an island near *Paumben*.

12. *Sílas and Charanas.*—The former are the five vows to abstain from —(1.) killing; (2.) stealing; (3.) fornication; (4.) lying; (5.) drinking intoxicating liquors. The *Charana* have been described *infra*. (*Vide* Note 5, Chap. I.)

13. *Kalyání.*—The present Calany, near Colombo, where there is a large Buddhistic temple. It is one of the great strongholds of modern Buddhism in Ceylon, and attracts a large number of

votaries." The word means "the happy. There are several places in India called *Kalyán.*

14. *Footprint.*—(*Vide* Note 7, Chap. II.)

15. *Díghavápi* means literally the long lake. It is supposed to be Batticaloa.

16. *Samapatti* means the enjoyment of *Samádhi* or meditation.

17. *Thúpáráma, Maháthúpa.*—The site of these monuments at Anuradhapura is even now known.

18. *Three times, i.e.,* the present, past, and future.

19. *Siláthúpa* is now called the *Gal-dágoba.*

20. *Acts of hospitality.*—Buddhist priests were strictly forbidden to avail themselves of the hospitality of friends, lest they may get attached to them. They were taught to be content with the little they obtained by begging.

21. *The religion of the Teacher, consisting of nine parts.*—These are (1.) *Sutta;* (2.) *Geyya;* (3.) *Vyákarana;* (4.) *Gáthá;* (5.) *Udána;* (6.) *Itivuttaka;* (7.) *Játaka;* (8.) *Abbhuta Dhamma;* (9.) *Vedallam.* (*Vide Majjhima Nikáya.*)

22. *Kusinárá.*—Supposed to be *Haridwar.*

23. *Sála-tree.*—*Shorea robusta,* called now *Hal*-tree.

24. *Malla kings.*—Supposed to be the kings of *Malava* or Malwa.

25. *The five-eyed one.*—Buddha, who had five kinds of eyes, viz.—(1.) Eyes of flesh; (2.) Divine eyes; (3.) Eyes of wisdom; (4.) The eye of a Buddha; (5.) The omniscient eye.

26. *First watch.*—There were three watches, as follow:—

The 1st watch	was from	6 P.M. to 10 P.M.
„ 2d	„	10 P.M. to 2 A.M.
„ 3d	„	2 A.M. to 6 A.M.

27. *Appamáda.*—Non-procrastination, zeal, diligence, &c.

28. *Jhána.*—(*Vide* note on *Samádhi,* Note 31, Chap. I.)—Is also a kind of religious meditation or reflection.

29. *Parinibbána.*—The pre-eminent *Nibbána.* The Sutta here referred to is Buddha's last discourse. It is held in the greatest veneration by the Buddhists, and would contrast favourably with other similar discourses. It is the Phædo of Buddhism. After it was delivered, Buddha ceased to exist. There is some hope of a translation of this being published soon.

30. *Coffin filled with oil.*—Even in the present day, when priests of eminence die, the corpse is placed in a coffin filled with oil, which is then burnt up. Sometimes melted butter is used instead of oil. As a rule, coffins are not used for purposes of cremation nowadays.

31. *The funeral pile* is a great institution in the East. Except those who died of the small-pox, all dead were burnt up amongst the Hindus, and the ashes thrown into a running stream. Sometimes sandal-wood was the firewood used for the funeral pile of the rich. It is curious to note that Sir H. Thompson should now so strongly advocate the extinction by fire of corpses—a custom adopted by the Hindus centuries ago—and this on scientific and economical grounds.

32. *Máha Kássapa.*—One of the first eighty disciples of Buddha. He presided at the first convocation. His biography can be learnt more fully from the thirteenth chapter of the *Chúla Vagga.*

33. *Fourfold Knowledge.*—These were—(1.) *Atthapatisambhidá*, or a clear perception of the *meaning* of things; (2.) *Dhammapatisambhida*, or a clear perception of the *nature* of things; (3.) *Niruttipati*, or knowledge of philology; and (4.) *Patibhánapati*, &c., a freedom from ignorance.

34. *Mahiyangana.*—(*Vide* Note 3.)

35. *Saññojana.*—(*Vide* Note 7, Chap. I.)

36. *Dona*, a convert to Buddhism referred to in *Parinibbána Sutta.* He is alleged to have composed 12,000 stanzas in praise of Buddha.

37. *Sakka.*—Indra.

38. *Gandhára.*—Supposed to be Candahar. But was this a Hindu state in ancient times?

39. *Brahmadatta, king of Kalinga.*—The former is a common name. *Kalinga* is the Northern *Circars.*

40. *Three gems.*—(*Vide* Note 8, Chap. I.)

41. *The requisites of worship.*—These were flowers, incense, lights, scents, offerings, &c.

42. *Adorned the heavenly assembly, i.e.*, became one of the denizens of heaven.

43. *Niganthas.*—A sect of *Sivites*, and formidable opponents of the Buddhists. They are also alleged to have been naked mendicants. Frequent allusions to this sect in Buddhistic writings show to what extent their tenets had once prevailed in India.

44. *Triumphal arches* would be the approximate rendering of *Thoranas.* These were often made movable, and of diverse cloths. They are in use up to the present day in India.

45. *The sea raging at the destruction of the world.*—One sign of the world's end, according to Hindu notion, would be the uproar caused by the waves of the sea.

46. *Síha panchara* is rendered by "windows." Possibly these had the images of lions to adorn them in ancient times. Hence the name.

47. *Pátaliputta* is modern Patna.

48. *Jambudípa*, another name for India. (*Vide* Note 22, Chap. I.)

49. *Siva, Brahma,* and *Vishnu* formed the Hindu triad, and were the principal gods of the Indian mythology.

50. *Worshipping the bone of a dead body.*—Nothing could be more opposed to Hindu faith. The very touch of a corpse was pollution to *Vishnuvites* and *Sivites.*

51. *Fourfold army,* or the *Chaturanga Sená*, consisted of—(1.) men; (2.) elephants; (3.) horses; and (4.) chariots. This is supposed to be the origin of chess, which is also called *Chaturanga* by the Hindus.

52. *Almsgiving halls.*—The Bishop-designate of Victoria, discoursing the other day on the defects of Buddhism, said that the Buddhists had no idea of charitable institutions. The allusion here shows that he was wrong. There was nothing more forcibly inculcated, both in Buddhism and the higher phases of Hinduism, than charity, whether it meant what St Paul taught it to be, or mere almsgiving, as the majority of the world deem it to consist of.

53. *Harichandanam* can be translated also as the yellow sandal-wood.

54. *Sea-monsters* would perhaps convey a correct idea of *Makara.*

55. *Tenfold power.*—(*Vide* Note 3, Chap. IV.)

56. *Gandamba.*—A mango-tree.

57. *Abhidhamma.*—(*Vide* Note 9, Chap. V.)

58. *Chámaras.*—(*Vide* Note 7, Chap. V.)

59. *Lokavivarana.*—A miracle by which one is enabled to see the entire world at once.

60. *Vissakamma.*—The name of the architect of the gods.

CHAPTER III.

1. *Market-towns.*—These were of less importance than cities. Buddhist writers always dwell upon this distinction between market-towns and cities, as if it were a matter of great consequence.

2. *Followed by the minds, though not by the bodies.*—This means that though the people themselves did not follow the king, yet their affections and thoughts did.

3. *Vases filled with scented water.*—This is a custom observed to the present day. Brass vases filled with water, and decorated with mango leaves and flowers, are placed near the door-posts and halls on all auspicious occasions.

4. *Dancing, singing, and instrumental music.*—These formed the three great accessories to all amusements in ancient India.
5. *Roruva.*—(*Vide* Note 60, Chap. I.)
6. *Kunda flower* was a species of jasmine.
7. *Janaddana* is another name for *Vishnu*, the second god of the Hindu triad.
8. *Ráma.*—An incarnation of *Vishnu*, or the hero of the great epic poem, Rámáyana.
9. *Náráyana* is also another name for *Vishnu*, more frequently used by the *Vishnuvites.*
10. *Sprinkled the relic with water.*—The Hindus perform all magical and holy rites by the sprinkling of water.
11. *The Omniscient, i.e.*, Buddha.
12. *Anáthapindappada* is a name frequently occurring in Buddhistic writings, and especially in *Sutta Nipáta.* He built the *Jetavana Vihára.*
13. *Jetavana.*—(*Vide* Note 8, Chap. II.)
14. *The four requisites* of a priest are—(1.) The yellow robes; (2.) The bowl for receiving food; (3.) Medicines; and (4.) Beds.
15. *Tathágata, i.e.*, Buddha.—(*Vide* Note 23, Chap. I.) From the 31st to the 52d verse, a brief account is given of the meritorious deeds of Buddha in his previous states of existence. To those acquainted with the legends connected with Buddha's life, the references here would be familiar. The object of the poet is to compress into a single stanza the history of a previous birth, and to show what self-sacrifices Gotama made for the benefit of all living creatures. He attained Buddhahood as the consummation of all the virtues he had practised before.
16. *Osadhi.*—The Ceylon Buddhists consider this to be Venus, or *Velli*, as he is called in Southern India, though some Orientalists think that *Osadhi* is only another name for the moon.
17. *Magical power.*—The Hindus made a distinction between magical powers which were founded on deception or the influence of evil spirits, and supernatural powers, which resulted from the pre-eminent virtues or merit of the person who called them into action.
18. *Nandá.*—A lake in *Indra loka*, or the kingdom of the gods.
19. *Five kinds of lotus, i.e.*, the blue, red, white, yellow, and golden.
20. *Who had modesty for their ornament, i.e.*, who were so bashful, that under other circumstances they would never have ventured to dance.
21. *Forests of water-lilies blossom.*—There are certain flowers, such as the lotus, which the Indian poets describe as opening out their flowers only at sunrise, whilst others only at the rise of the moon. The sun is thus called "the lord of the lotus," and

the moon that of other flowers, like the lily, &c. (*Vide* also Note 12, Chap. V.)

22. *Kappina, Bimbisára, Suddhodana, &c.*—These were eminent kings of India. The second was a very powerful monarch, who reigned during the lifetime of Gotama Buddha at *Rájagaha*, and was ultimately slain by his son, *Ajasat.*

23. *The thousand-eyed, i.e.*, Indra, who was alleged to have a thousand eyes, which, in truth, were the transformations of a thousand defects which the curse of a sage whom he had offended had brought upon him.

24. *Champac flower, i.e.*, the flower of *Michelia champaca.*

25. *Mandákiní* is a celestial river, taking its rise in Mount *Meru.*

26. *The right side turned towards it.*—By the Hindus the right side was deemed the propitious side.

CHAPTER IV.

1. *The king of lions, though it saw a mighty elephant.*—Indian poets consider elephants the special victims of lions, and these are supposed to have a special *penchant* for the slaughter of those huge animals. One legend says that a lioness never delivers herself of her young one till she has come within sight of an elephant, for it is considered necessary that the little cub, as soon as it sees light, should spring on such a monster and kill him. The frequent allusions to lions in Indian writings show that Indian forests must have once abounded with lions.

2. *Ujjéní.*—Modern Oojein.

3. *Him possessed of the ten powers, i.e.*, Buddha, who is possessed of ten powers, *i.e.*, ten powers of wisdom.

4. *Hemamálá* means literally a chain of gold.

5. *Malaya.*—Possibly it means *Malayála* or Travancore.

6. *Mahásena.*—One of the last kings mentioned in the *Mahawansa.* He forms the connecting-link between this book and the *Suluvansa.*

7. *Southern country.*—Southern India.

8. *Thera.*—An elderly saint or priest.

9. *The son of the Sage, i.e.*, the *Thera.* Priests are called the sons of Buddha. As to *husband and wife*, consult Note 1, Chap. V.

10. *Meru.*—The chief of mountains, supposed to be in the centre of the universe.

11. *Ratanagiri.*—The mountain of gems, the same as *Meru.*—*Garula* is a large specimen of the Brahman kite, a bird supposed to be ridden by *Vishnu*, and is the recognised enemy of all snakes.

12. *The right of ruling the entire circle of the earth* is the rendering adopted for *Rajjalakkhyiam*, which is equal to the *Rájalakshmi* of the Hindus. It may be translated also as "the prosperity of ruling."
13. *Támalitti.*—A port on the Indian Ocean, supposed to be situated on one of the mouths of the Ganges.
14. *The kanduppala.*—A species of flower.
15. *Sadhu* means expressions of approval, somewhat like "Amen." "Be it so" is the literal meaning of the word.
16. *Massed hair.*—Or the top-knot hair of the head.
17. *The city of Lanká*, or *Lankapatanam*, is believed by some to be the present *Mantotte* in Ceylon; others think it to be a town now submerged.

CHAPTER V.

1. *Husband and wife* is an Oriental idiom, not unknown to the Sanskrit.
2. *Anurádhapura.*—The ancient capital of Ceylon, the ruins of which yet attract visitors. It was a city of great dimensions, inhabited by a numerous population.
3. *Directions and intermediate points.*—These were the four cardinal points, and those intermediate between them, being in all eight *Disá* or directions.
4. *Meghagiri.*—A monastery and temple to the north of *Anurádhapura.* The word literally means the "cloud hill."
5. *Chakka gem.*—One of the seven precious articles belonging to an universal monarch or *Chakkavatti.*
6. *Expounder of omens.*—The expounding of omens forms a distinct art amongst the Hindus. There are many books on the subject.
7. *Chámara.*—The tail of a yak wafted before kings, as one of the insignia of royalty. They are used also in the temples now.
8. *Delightful owing to the ripening of merit in the course of time.*—Or delightful owing to the varieties of change taking place in the course of time.
9. *Tipitaka.*—The well-known Buddhistic scriptures, consisting of three divisions, the *Sutta*, the *Vinaya*, and the *Abhidhamma.*—*Játaka.*—The legends relating to Buddha's births, replete with much curious and interesting information relating to ancient India.—*Ágama.*—The four *Nikayas* are called *Agámas* by the Buddhists, but amongst the Hindus the term is used for an extensive department of *Saiva Saddhántic* scriptures but little known as yet to European scholars. Their great propounder was *Sankaráchárya.*

10. *Mokkha.*—Equal to *mukti* or *moksha* (Sanskrit), heaven. It literally means "release," *i.e.*, release from births.

11. *Nikáyas.*—These were three monasteries or societies, viz.—*Mahágiri*, *Abhayagiri*, and *Dhammaruchi.*

12. *Quickly opened the multitude of lotus faces.*—Indian poets compare human faces to lotus flowers, which expand and close their petals respectively at the rising and setting of the sun. Here the king is compared to the sun, and is supposed to have cheered up the drooping spirits of his people by his coming among them, as the sun, by its morning rays, expands the lotus flowers.

13. *Rows of plantain-trees.*—With these even now the streets are decorated on festive occasions.

14. *Vases filled with water.*—(*Vide* Note 3, Chap. III.)

15. *Chief* is the rendering of *Tilaka*, which means the pre-eminent. It is generally employed to designate the sectarian mark used by the Hindus on their foreheads.

16. *Migadáya.*—Another name for *Isipatana*, so called because cattle roamed there without any danger.

17. *Mahinda.*—Son of King *Asoka*, and the saint who first propounded Buddhism in Ceylon, where he landed, Anno Buddha 237.

18. *Abhayuttara.*—The same as *Abhayagiri.* (*Vide* Note 11 above.)

19. *Buddhadása*—An eminent and good king who flourished about 882 of the Buddhist era. He ordered that every village should have a priest and a surgeon, so that both the souls and the bodies of his people might be equally well looked after. He was also the author of a medical work.

THE HISTORY OF THE AUTHOR.

1. (6) The order of the verses in this chapter is deranged for the purpose of rendering the translation intelligible. This serves to show in some respects the natural sequence of ideas and the peculiar construction of sentences in Eastern languages.

2. *Tiká* means a commentary. The name of this commentary on the commentary called *Panchika* for the grammar of *Chandagomi* is *Ratanamati.*

3. *Anguttara* is the name of a *Nikayo,* the fourth division of the *Suttapitaka.*

4. *Sáriputta* lived at *Pollanaruva* at the time of *Prakkrama Báhu I.*

5. *All the various systems of religions.*—Their number once in India must have been a legion, expressing all shades of thought and faith, from the grossest Epicureanism to the most subtle Transcendentalism.

APPENDIX.

An Extract from Mr Fergusson's work on Indian Art, showing that Dantapura was on the site of modern Jugganauth.

A GREAT deal of speculation has been afloat regarding the origin of the worship of Jugganauth at *Puri*, which differs in many respects from that paid to the Hindu deities in general; and it has been more than once surmised that many of its peculiarities are borrowed from Buddhism, which I believe to be the correct view of the case. In the first place, I think there can be little doubt but that the temple itself now occupies the site where formerly stood the dagoba containing the celebrated tooth-relic. Certain it is that there is no other spot in the neighbourhood where any trace of it can be found; and a dagoba is such a solid mass of materials, that, except in the neighbourhood of a large city, it would be difficult to obliterate all traces of it; and the mass of materials, or earth, that it would take to fill up the terrace on which the temple stands, looks very like such an accumulation, and very unlike any work of the twelfth century, when nothing of the kind was ever attempted that I know of. Almost all writers mention the tradition of a relic being contained in the image itself; some call it a bone, some say that it is only a piece of the old image, which is periodically renewed; but, whatever it is, the idea of any relic is so totally foreign to the whole system of Hinduism, and so essentially a part of Buddhism, that I cannot but think it strongly confirmatory of this view of the case. If it is a bone, it probably pretends to be the tooth-relic that plays so important a part in Indian history.* The absence of caste at these festivals is a third characteristic of Buddhism, not found elsewhere in Hindostan at the present day, nor, perhaps, more than nominally here; but the fact of its being admitted by the Brahmans, is an acknowledgment of a Buddhist doctrine too important to be overlooked.

---

* Indeed, the image itself appears to be in form a sort of compromise between a Buddhist dagoba, a relic-shrine, and the human form in ordinary Hindu deities, and certainly unlike any other god or mortal the world ever saw.

THE END.